Persuading the Cretans

Persuading the Cretans

A Text-Generated Persuasion Analysis of the Letter to Titus

ALDRED A. GENADE

WIPF & STOCK · Eugene, Oregon

PERSUADING THE CRETANS
A Text-Generated Persuasion Analysis of the Letter to Titus

Copyright © 2011 Aldred A. Genade. All rights reserved. Except for brief quotations in critical publications or reviews, no part of this book may be reproduced in any manner without prior written permission from the publisher. Write: Permissions, Wipf and Stock Publishers, 199 W. 8th Ave., Suite 3, Eugene, OR 97401.

Unless otherwise noted, Scripture quotations in the body of the analysis are that of the author or are from the Revised Standard Version of the Bible, ©1946 (renewed 1973), 1956, and 1971 by the Division of Christian Education of the National Council of the Churches of Christ in the United States of America. Used by permission.

Wipf & Stock
An Imprint of Wipf and Stock Publishers
199 W. 8th Ave., Suite 3
Eugene, OR 97401

www.wipfandstock.com

ISBN 13: 978-1-60899-330-7

Manufactured in the U.S.A.

To my darling mother.
To some you are Sheila, to others Marie; to me you'll always be Moeksie.
Your company that month and a half in Potch meant
more than you will know.

Contents

Preface ... ix
Acknowledgments ... xi
1 Introduction ... 1
2 Titus 1:1–4 ... 14
3 Titus 1:5–9 ... 22
4 Titus 1:10–16 ... 29
5 Titus 2:1 ... 40
6 Titus 2:2–10 ... 43
7 Titus 2:11–15 ... 55
8 Titus 3:1–2 ... 67
9 Titus 3:3 ... 74
10 Titus 3:4–7 ... 80
11 Titus 3:8–11 ... 99
12 Titus 3:12–15 ... 107
13 Conclusion ... 113
Appendix ... 123
Bibliography ... 131

Preface

ALL SCIENTIFIC ENDEAVORS PRESUPPOSE community and interdependence. As in life, so in biblical studies, no one is an island. This is true of me and of the contribution to the study of Titus I am hereby making. My contribution is neither a panacea nor is it infallible. Its uniqueness (weakness) lies in the assumption of the author's intention to persuade as well as its exclusive focus upon the Letter to Titus. The methodology experimented with here was developed by my dissertation supervisor, D. F. Tolmie. My first exposure to it was during my PhD studies. Since then, I've reconsidered the method and have improvements to suggest. In this book, I will suggest a more descriptive name, which I submit as *text-generated persuasion analysis* rather than *text-centered rhetorical analysis*. In future publications, I plan to suggest a systemization for the method.

Those looking for the definitive answer to the authorship question in these pages look in vain. This matter is taken up in numerous other volumes, articulated by greater minds than mine. My concern is primarily the persuasive structure of the letter. I do hold, for various reasons, to Pauline authorship of Titus as well as of the Timothean correspondence.

This project did not start off because I wanted to "prove" anything, but by default I do present some new ideas about the structure of the text: that there is a multilayered structure and that the letter proves to be coherent. Rhetorical studies have come a long way, and together with other analytical tools, it holds the promise of aiding our appreciation for the "power of the text."

Acknowledgments

Through my journey with this letter, I traversed many curves and hairpin bends, and sometimes even did a little off-roading. Without help along the way, I would not have completed this project. Now, I have the opportunity to thank those who helped me.

Help came first in the form of my *Doktorvater*, D. F. Tolmie, dean of the Faculty of Theology, University of the Free State. He guided and encouraged me and became a friend.

I would also like to thank:

The Tuesday night small group, "Bible-study friends" from the Reformed Church Potchefstroom (North), for nudging me and holding me accountable when I requested prayer support for the project, especially Jeanette.

The Wednesday night home-fellowship group from Ubuntu Family Center, Promosa, for their concern and support in prayer; for their patience in having to meet without me for several weeks as I worked toward completion. Fazel, Alastair, Melanie, and Taryn, thank you!

My current dean, colleague and friend, Fika Janse van Rensburg, New Testament professor, North-West University (NWU), for constant encouragement, but mostly for modeling industriousness, excellence, and passion.

The faculty and staff of the NWU Theology Department, especially At Lamprecht, for asking me daily, without fail, "Is die boek al klaar?" (Is the book done yet?) The dread of seeing him and having to answer that question played no small part in my haste to finish!

Friends and neighbors at Denne Park (you know who you are—clue Jamaican and Dutch), for encouraging me to "get it done!"

Most importantly, to our great God and Savior, Jesus Christ, who died to save a wretch like me, who in spite of my countless weaknesses graces me to serve him by enabling me to complete what was started. *Soli Deo gloria!*

1

Introduction

The Cinderella Letter

From the Shadows to the Stage

THIS IS A BOOK about the Letter to Titus. It is not a commentary in the popular sense of the word. Utilizing a modified *rhetorical* critical model, it analyzes the argumentative or persuasive tapestry that comprises the text of this letter; it presupposes that the author[1] like a consummate weaver, has woven an intricate, yet charming and delightful masterpiece. An exquisite textual fabric, which Martin Luther esteems "a model of Christian doctrine, in which is comprehended in a masterful way all that is necessary for a Christian to know and to live."[2] Such high and exclusive regard is absent from most contemporary appraisals of

---

1. The rationale for rejecting Pauline authorship of Titus is far from convincing. The arguments of those scholars who accept the traditional view on authorship of the Pastoral Letters are sustained. See in this regard Witherington, *Letters and Homilies*; Mounce, *Pastoral Epistles*; Knight, *Pastoral Epistles*. I concede the complexity of the debate and caution that humility should be the benchmark in our differences on this matter (see the advice of Achtemeier et al., *Introducing the New Testament*, 464). However, it will become obvious that the identity of the author is of little consequence for the analysis performed in this volume. Accordingly, the self-identification of the author in 1:1 as "Paul" prevails. My own analysis is motivated in part by the recognition that the letter has its own *voice* and can stand on its own. Like Johnson, I too believe that if scholars evaluated the letters individually first, and then compared them with the rest of the Pauline corpus, the conclusions on pseudonymity would stand on shaky ground (Johnson, *Paul's Delegates*, 7; Carson and Moo, *Introduction*, 555).

2. Luther, "St. Paul to Titus," 389.

Titus, especially in the academic realm.[3] Also absent is a comprehensive analysis of the structure of the letter, independent of 1 and 2 Timothy and without approaching it in terms of the pervasive authenticity/inauthenticity debate. This book sets out to do just that. The implication is that Titus has not been approached in this way before. A cursory review of the status of the letter will show how the conclusion that the independence of Titus is underappreciated is legitimate and will provide the necessary context for the hypothesis.

What is the status of this letter in current scholarship? It has, as least in academic circles, for a long time, taken the back seat in virtually all discussions of the popularly denoted Pastoral Epistles. Under the influence of the notorious authenticity debate,[4] the Timothean correspondence

---

3. The most comprehensive and reputable single-volume commentary dedicated to Titus is probably Quinn, *Letter to Titus*.

4. The issue of authorship is undoubtedly the dominant contention in regard to the Pastorals. Scholarship is generally divided into two camps. At the one end of the spectrum, there are those who maintain that the letters were authored by Paul, in accordance with the self-identification of the letter. Scholars at the opposite end maintain that these letters are later non-Pauline or pseudonymous creations. Until the turn of the nineteenth century, the authenticity of the Pastoral Letters was unchallenged. Subsequently, there followed a succession of dissident voices, mainly from Germany, that snowballed into the present polarity on this issue. The works of Friedrich Schleiermacher, *Über Den Ersten Brief Pauli an Timotheus*, and Ferdinand Christian Bauer, *Die Sogennanten Pastoralbriefe Des Apostels Paulus*, circulate as the original catalysts in what has become the authenticity debate. The grounds upon which the authenticity of the letters is considered spurious relate primarily to linguistic and stylistic discrepancies.

The rejection of the authenticity of all three letters occurred rapidly though not automatically. In this regard, it is interesting to note how early scholars contradicted each other; some accepted the authenticity of one letter while rejecting the rest, and vice versa. During the early church era, Tatian rejected 1 and 2 Timothy but accepted the Letter to Titus as authentically Pauline. See Dibelius and Conzelmann, *Pastoral Epistles*, 2. The same ambivalence is noticeable among early German scholars. One questioned whether 1 Timothy could have been written by the same author who penned the other two (see Schmidt, *Historisch Kritische Einleitung*). Another doubted that Titus came from the hand of Paul, but upheld the authenticity of the Timothean correspondence (Evanson, *Dissonance of the Four*, 318–19). Even Schleiermacher, consistently identified as the pioneer of the debate, accepted only the authenticity of Titus and 2 Timothy. By 1812, however, the authenticity of all three Pastorals would be rejected (Eichorn, *Einleitung*).

Contemporary defenders of Pauline authorship include: Knight, *Pastoral Epistles*; Towner, *Timothy and Titus*; Johnson, *Paul's Delegates*; Mounce, *Pastoral Epistle*; Dunn, *Letters to Timothy*; Köstenberger, "Challenges"; Van Neste, "Message." Recent proponents of non-Pauline authorship include: Harding, *Tradition and Rhetoric*; Collins, *Timothy and Titus*; Marshall et al., *Exploring*; Marshall, " 'I Left You in Crete.' " Thus, we see respected scholars on both sides of the debate approaching the matter of au-

enjoyed the spotlight while Titus was (unwittingly) banished to the academic backwaters.[5] However, modifications of this trend are on the rise, with several contributions investigating, for example, the theology[6] and other aspects of the letter.[7] These suggest tentative, though overdue, steps toward appreciating the independence and individuality of Titus.[8]

---

thorship as something not to be regarded lightly. The complexity of the debate has been succinctly summarized by Quinn: "All scholars of the PE draw inferences from practically the same concrete data in and about the letters, analysing the linguistic, historico-sociological, and theological components of the correspondence. Yet, these data have provoked the most dramatically different hypotheses to explain the origin and purpose of the PE" (*Letter to Titus*, 17). See Witherington, *Letters and Homilies*, 58ff. for an interesting hypothesis of a Pauline-Lukan collaboration in the authorship of the Pastorals.

5. The link between the authorship debate and the evident neglect of the Pastoral Epistles generally and Titus specifically is beyond dispute. With reference to the latter, it could be argued that Titus is doubly neglected. In relation to the rest of New Testament studies, the Pastorals as a corpus are considered marginalized. Next, Titus is deemed neglected *within* the corpus. By 1989, these three letters had all but disappeared from the radar of academic interest (see Epp and MacRae, eds., *New Testament*; Johnson, *Paul's Delegates*, 4–5). The peripherization of the Pastorals continued into the nineties. The Pretoria conference on Rhetoric, Scripture and Theology of 1994 has no contributions dealing with the Pastorals, yet the index discloses three pages of references to the early Christian writings and the classical authors. See in this regard Porter and Olbricht, *Rhetoric, Scripture and Theology*. Another 1994 academic collection has absolutely zero references to Titus but at least one to 1 and 2 Timothy (Lambrecht, *Pauline Studies*, 464).

6. This shift was first applied to the three letters collectively. A 2004 survey of research on the Pastorals highlighted this trend, from authorship issues to a focus upon the text itself, "its theology, rhetoric, and reception" (McKnight and Osborne, *Face of New Testament Studies*, 292). Unfortunately, it only cites research addressing literary aspects of the Timothean correspondence. Thus, the individuality of the Timothean letters was the first to get some attention.

Investigations into the theology of Titus have focused on particular verses, for example the Christologically significant Titus 2:13. In this regard see Smith and Song, "Some Christological Implications"; Bowman, "Jesus Christ, God Manifest"; Fee, *Pauline Christology*. More comprehensive studies include Karris, *Symphony*; Thurston, "Theology of Titus"; Hagner, "Titus as a Pauline Letter"; Collins, "Epistle to Titus."

7. See Wieland, "Roman Crete," which proposes the plausibility and actuality of Crete. For the Roman background to Titus see Gill, "Cities of Crete." The structure and purpose of the letter gets a fresh take in Tollefson, "Revitalization"; Wieland, "Grace Manifest"; and Kidd, "Titus as Apologia." See also Smith, "Criss-Cross Chiasmus;" and Clark, "Discourse Structure." Titus 1:12, known as the liar's paradox, continues to tantalize scholars. See Gray, "Liar Paradox."

8. The call is for scholars to consider the three letters individually rather than as a corpus. See Johnson, *Paul's Delegates*, 7; Van Neste, "Structure," 121; and Davies, *Pastoral Epistles*, 90.

The battle for the heart of Titus's independence and integrity has shifted to the domain of literary structure. Simply, is Titus a coherent text or not? Judging from the deafening clang of swords in the academic arena, the answer is not obvious. A spillover from the authorship debate, scholars maintain one of two positions, either that Titus does not[9] or does[10] indeed cohere structurally. James Miller represents the former view. In *The Pastoral Letters as Composite Documents*, he concludes that "the [Pastoral] letters have no driving concern, no consistent focus of interest; instead, they read like an anthology of traditions, many arranged mechanically together by topic, some simply juxtaposed."[11] His appraisal of the salutation of Titus is equally uncomplimentary; he deems it "notoriously complicated and confusing."[12] Ray van Neste[13] responded to Miller's challenging hypothesis. By examining what he calls the "linguistic cohesiveness"[14] of Titus, he proposes three ways in which cohesion is facilitated, namely cohesion shifts, transitional devices, and repetitions.[15] Thus, Miller's composite letter hypothesis leads him back to the authenticity/inauthenticity issue. It is not the work of a single author, much less of Paul.[16] Van Neste's defense of the letter's compositional integrity assuages his own apprehension that the theological integrity and value of Titus risk being compromised.[17] These two positions are at odds in terms of objectives, outcomes, scope, comprehensiveness, and methodologies.[18] Miller's focus is not exclusively upon Titus, while Van Neste is limited by virtue of writing a journal article with its concomitant restrictions.

---

9. See Van Neste, "Structure," 119. He avers that the coherence of Titus is the majority view. Yet, even Guthrie, who defends Pauline authorship, judges the letters to evince a "lack of studied order, some subjects being treated more than once in the same letter without apparent premeditation," and concludes that they are "far removed from literary exercises." See Guthrie, *Pastoral Epistles*, 12.

10. For coherency of the Pastorals generally see Towner, *Goal*; Donelson, *Pseudipigraphy*; Fiore, *Personal Example*; and Verner, *Household*.

11. Miller, "Composite Documents," 138.

12. Ibid., 124.

13. Van Neste, "Structure," 118–33.

14. Ibid., 121.

15. Ibid., 122–26, 126–27, and 127–30, respectively.

16. Miller, "Composite Documents," 141–42.

17. Van Neste, "Structure," 120, 130.

18. Van Neste utilizes a discourse analytical model. See Ibid., 118. Miller uses "compositional analysis." See Miller, "Composite Documents," 124.

Stalemate! There appears, therefore, to be an opportunity, if not a need, to clarify this matter by means of focusing exclusively upon the Titus letter and utilizing an appropriate tool for analyzing it. I respectfully disagree with the finality implied by Miller's conclusions: that the letters and Titus in particular lack compositional integrity. I find myself rather in sympathy with Van Neste that a vacuum exists: "Thus, the tasks of tracing the *flow of argument* in *each* letter and of noting the *overarching coherence* of *each* letter remain to be done."[19] This book is an attempt to advance the dialogue concerning the macrostructural coherence of Titus in a meaningful way. The instrument that will be employed toward this end is a modified rhetorical critical method. Since my method differs from conventional rhetorical criticism, appreciating its distinctiveness necessitates a review of recent rhetorical analyses of Titus. Two contemporary treatises are in circulation, one by Carl Joachim Classen, the other by Ben Witherington III. That these exist is a miracle; that they are so few testifies to the isolated status of the letter.

On Broadway: Rhetorical Studies of Titus

Carl Joachim Classen's "Improvisational" Rhetorical Reading

In 2002, C. J. Classen put forth an analysis of the rhetoric of Titus.[20] A pioneering contribution, this contemporary rhetorical analysis or "reading" introduces a fresh methodological approach. It discards with the rigid application of classic rhetorical categories[21] and advocates the liberal employment of contemporary rhetorical innovations.[22] His basic premise is that a rhetorical analysis or "reading" of a letter like Titus can be done without slavish adherence to the strictures of preexisting classical categories.[23] By paying careful and exclusive attention to the language, Classen argues, one can disclose authorial intention, literary structure, and the nature of the letter. Consequently, he defines

---

19. Van Neste, "Structure," 120. Emphasis added.

20. Classen, "Rhetorical Reading"; Classen, *Rhetorical Criticism*, 45–67.

21. Classen refrains from categorizing the text according to classic rhetorical genres like deliberative, epideictic, and forensic rhetoric. Neither does he divide the text using the categories like *exordium, narratio, propositio*, and *probatio*.

22. Classen, *Rhetorical Criticism*, 27.

23. Ibid., 48: "not to analyze . . . with the help of handbooks of rhetoric or epistolography . . . or on the basis of preconceived ideas and categories."

"rhetoric" as "the deliberate calculated use of *language* for the sake of communicating various kinds of information in the manner intended by the speaker (and the theory of such use)," with language being "the essential element."[24] He adds that "an element of deliberation, of systematization and of planning seems to me to be an essential characteristic of rhetoric."[25] He explains rhetorical reading as "reading a text in order to grasp the information it intends to impart, to understand its meaning or its message by appreciating and explaining the function of every single part of it as well as of the composition as a whole. [It] means reading a text as composed by an authoress or an author with the particular intention of addressing a particular audience or individual at a particular moment or a wider public (wider both with regard to space and time) and, therefore, formulated in a carefully considered manner."[26] Classen understands three aspects to be materially significant. First, there is the text itself; next, the relationship between author and audience as discernable from the text; and finally, the structure of the text. The result is the following outline in its broadest division:

a. 1:1–4: Salutation

b. 1:5–13a: The mandate to Titus, the qualifications for eldership, and the characterization of the opponents

c. 1:13b–2:15: A general order for Titus: to show the Cretans the paths to sound belief

d. 3:1–7: A further order with regard to specific aspects with justifications

e. 3:8–11: Summary of 1:5–3:7 with admonitions, promises, and warnings to the audience

f. 3:12–14: Particular instructions

g. 3:15: Final greetings

This groundbreaking approach has several distinct features. It largely avoids cataloging the letter according to ancient rhetorical theory[27] since it is essentially text centered. He identifies ancient rhetorical ele-

---

24. Ibid., 45–46. Emphasis added.
25. Ibid., 46.
26. Ibid.
27. See ibid., 65.

ments *after* his analysis, and only those that would seem to be present. Thus, he defines as *inventio* those ideas the author wants to develop; as *dispositio*, the relationship between various ideas and their respective importance; as *rhetorical situation*, the intended reception of the ideas by the audience. Rather than isolating Titus, the analysis proceeds by comparison with the authentic Pauline corpus. The distribution of imperatives (1:13, 2:1, 2:6, 2:15, 3:1, 3:9, 3:10) defines the nature of the letter as one "with instructions, mandates, injunctions, admonitions and warnings."[28] Classen's analysis of Titus exemplifies a trendsetting adaptation of rhetorical theory to explain the structure, nature, and contents of an epistolary text. The unorthodoxy of Classen's approach has not escaped evaluation, nor should it be allowed to.

The study invites both praise and pummeling. Its significance is multifaceted. Foremost is the priority it places upon the letter, namely paying exclusive attention to Titus. Demonstrating the efficacy of rhetorical criticism, albeit unconventional criticism, to explain the "eccentricities" of Titus adds to the study's weight. The initiative to structure and define the nature of the letter around the distribution of imperatives is rather novel, if not exceptional. On the whole, this study suggests some coherent structure for Titus, its individual parts deliberately and calculatedly selected for their contribution toward the author's objective.[29]

Scientific endeavor, however, demands not only laudation where it is due but also critical observation. The shortcomings of the study are several, ranging from the benign to the more severe. One critic considers it methodologically below par, calling it "quasi-rhetorical."[30] While it seems a highly subjective, almost arbitrary method, it assorts rather well with Classen's innovative bent. He advocates with reference to rhetorical categories that "one should not hesitate to use the most developed and sophisticated form, as it will offer more help than any other."[31]

Furthermore, this is not a comprehensive treatment of the whole letter. Several words and parts of sentences are left unexplained.[32] Instead

---

28. Ibid., 55, 60.

29. Ibid., 65, 66.

30. Witherington, *Letters and Homilies*, 91.

31. Classen, *Rhetorical Criticism*, 5. This harmonizes with a trend he observes in the work of Philip Melanchthon (11).

32. E.g., he does not say anything about the following words in 1:2 and 1:3, namely ἣν ἐπηγγείλατο and ἐν κηρύγματι, ὃ ἐπιστεύθην ἐγώ, respectively (cf. 2:2, Πρεσβύτας

of regarding this as an oversight, it could be attributable to the intent to merely demonstrate the methodology by employing Titus as a test sample due to its relative brevity. In other words, comprehensive analysis might never have been intended.

One critical lapse in the article concerns the inattention given to persuasion, a fundamental aspect of rhetorical criticism.[33] The question should be asked, "*Why* does the author say what he is saying in the way he says it?"[34] The investigation simply highlights *what* is there in the text. It never proceeds to answer the next question, namely, *why* is it there? Leading on from this is, perhaps, a more serious defect of the study.

The interpretation tends to be more exegetical than rhetorical. It busies itself with the contents of the text but pays no attention to motive. The peculiarity of the vocabulary, unique phraseology, and syntactical considerations attract a fair amount of attention. What is not adequately explored is the *role* or *function* of the unique vocabulary and what the unusual syntax communicates about the intention of the author. Overall, this study concentrates on the linguistic aspects of the text rather than upon its rhetoric or persuasive intent.[35]

Ben Witherington III's Socio-Rhetorical Analysis

Witherington's commentary is an in invaluable contribution to the study of Titus.[36] A purported socio-rhetorical commentary, it locates the letter within the socioreligious environment of Hellenistic Christianity.[37]

. . . σώφρονας; 2:6–10a, Τοὺς νεωτέρους . . . ἐνδεικνυμένους ἀγαθήν; 3: 2, μηδένα . . . πραΰτητα).

33. See Du Toit, "Vilification," where he states, "We have too long neglected the fact that in one way or another each of these writings seeks to persuade *its readers/audience in a certain direction*. To ask what a New Testament text is *doing* is at least as important as asking what it is *saying*" (403, first emphasis added; second and third emphasis in the original). See Tolmie, *Persuading the Galatians*, 1. See also Du Toit, "Persuasion," 192. Cf. Hester (Amador), "Wuellnerian Sublime," 10, who maintains that rhetorics focus upon textual effect.

34. How does a text work to influence thought and action? Cf. D'Angelo, "Rhetorical Criticism," 604.

35. This fact is evident from his definition of rhetoric and rhetorical reading (see Classen, 45, 46). The emphasis seems to lie upon "understanding" the message, while "appreciating" and "explaining the function" of the parts as well as the whole composition. On page 63, he confesses that his method is deliberately linguistic.

36. Witherington, *Letters and Homilies*.

37. Vernon Robbins is the originator of socio-rhetorical criticism. Witherington

The rhetorical scope of the letter comes into play throughout the commentary. For example, the presence of rhythm, rhyme, assonance, and alliteration recognized in 1:5–9 suggests "a document that is a surrogate for oral and face-to-face instructions."[38] The overall rhetorical objective or "compositional goal" is "to highlight two competing lifestyles in the church and to plead for one and polemicize against the other."[39] This is achieved through a network of contrasts and comparisons or *synkrisis*.[40] This objective is partially tenable, but it is not necessarily the only one. In fact, one can safely argue for multiple rhetorical objectives, discernable at macro- as well as microstructural levels. This will be elaborated upon later.

Several unique features distinguish this contribution by Witherington. Among other things, this outstanding commentary contains multiple schematic outlines of arguments found in the letter.[41] These schematizations bolster evidence for the coherency of the letter.

Witherington avers that the letter addresses Titus rather than a congregation.[42] Why must it be either-or? Why can't it be both? The letter would have been read aloud, a reality Witherington is cognizant of since he acknowledges the presence of oral-aural structures in the text.[43] Furthermore, would Titus, whom Witherington decorates as a "crisis intervention specialist,"[44] require the level of persuasion evident in the text?

The outline communicates very little if nothing of the rhetorical import of the letter, although the author does pay attention to the rhetorical strategies throughout his analysis of the text. Still, the layout comes up short in terms of comprehensiveness and congruence to the actual rhetorical development characteristic of this letter. In fact, it resembles that of commentaries that do not necessarily claim to be rhetorical in nature, as can be seen below:

---

does not adhere to the strictures and categories of the discipline but employs socio-rhetorical criticism in a more generic manner so that it cannot *strictu sensu* be considered as socio-rhetorical.

38. Witherington, *Letters and Homilies*, 107.
39. Ibid., 96.
40. Ibid., 93, 127.
41. Ibid., 119, 130, 153.
42. Ibid., 92.
43. See n. 37 in this chapter.
44. Ibid., 88.

a. 1:1–4: Epistolary prescript
b. 1:5–9: Minding one's elders
c. 1:10–16: Rebuking the rebels
d. 2:1–15: Teaching tips for Titus on behavior and belief
e. 3:1–11: More orders from headquarters
f. 3:12–15: Travel plans and epistolary closing

The above scholars share methodological and terminological commonalities. Both deviate from "established" methodologies, abandoning classical rhetorical models. Classen is self-admittedly innovative while Witherington applies socio-rhetorical criticism relatively loosely. In this regard, they share an innovative streak. Terminologically, however, both tie the words "rhetoric" or "rhetorical" to their respective models yet attach different meanings to it. Thus, utilizing these terms of reference appears problematic.

The escalating ambiguity of the label "rhetorical criticism" seems to undermine its usefulness. Contemporary scholars used the term initially with reference to the application of Aristotelian or *classic* rhetorical categories to biblical texts,[45] but this practice has since become progressively unfashionable.[46] As early as the 1970s, the state of rhetorical scholarship in humanities and behavioral sciences was considered ambivalent or chaotic.[47] By 2002, *varieties* of rhetorical criticisms would be tagged as "modern," "antimodern," and "transmodern."[48] It seems increasingly appropriate nowadays to speak of "rhetorical criticisms"[49] and of "rhetorics" since "no one rhetorical critical theory is sufficient to unpack the meaning of a rhetorical artifact, especially when those artifacts are the texts of the New Testament."[50] To complicate the matter further, today,

---

45. This approach was epitomized by two pioneering authors, namely Kennedy, *New Testament*; and Betz, *Galatians*. See also Orton and Anderson, eds., *Literary Rhetoric*.

46. Cf. D'Angelo, *Rhetorical Criticism*, 605, 607; Classen, *Rhetorical Criticism*, 27; Olbricht, "Rhetorical Criticism," 27; Porter, "Theoretical Justification," 107–8; Anderson, *Rhetorical Theory*, 26; Tolmie, *Persuading the Galatians*, 24–26. See also Robbins's synoptic paper, "Rhetorical Analysis." It is an excellent summary and illustration of developments in the area of *rhetorical criticism*.

47. Becker, "Rhetorical Scholarship," 3.

48. Robbins, "Rhetorical Analysis," 17.

49. D'Angelo, *Rhetorical Criticism*, 605, speaks of a "plurality of critical methods."

50. Hester and Hester, *Rhetorics and Hermeneutics*, x. See also D'Angelo, "Rhetorical

one person's "rhetorical criticism" is another's "literary criticism" and vice versa.[51] Where does this leave us?

Rhetorical criticism is in a dynamic state of flux—it is evolving. The way forward is innovation and amalgamation. No, invention: "We need to *invent* a rhetorical criticism that is consonant with biblical discourse,"[52] "*creating* a universal grammar of rhetoric."[53] Closer to home, this raises the question of methodology to be followed in the analysis of Titus. For reasons presented above, the methodology of this study will not be the Greco-Roman system but a modification of a model developed by Pauline scholar, D. F. Tolmie.

Titus and Methodological Invention

From Tolmie's "Minimal Theory Framework" to "Text-Generated Persuasion Analysis"

In 2005, Tolmie was the first South African New Testament scholar to break allegiance with rhetorical analysis based upon the Greco-Roman model.[54] His *minimal theory framework* opened new possibilities for "other Pauline (and New Testament) letters."[55]

This method aims to reconstruct the author's rhetorical strategy from the text itself and involves a text-centered descriptive analysis of the way in which an author attempts to persuade the audience. A fundamental assumption is that biblical authors wrote with this intention to persuade. Thus, Tolmie views rhetoric as the employment of a text for the purpose of persuasion.[56] The methodology involves several steps,[57] set out below as sequential only for the sake of an orderly presentation, although he does not present it so.

Criticism," 605: "there is no single or correct method that can be applied to all texts."

51. D'Angelo, "Rhetorical Criticism," 604; see also Wuellner, "Where?" 451, 453.
52. Olbricht, "Rhetorical Criticism," 27. Emphasis added.
53. Anderson, *Rhetorical Theory*, 26. Emphasis added.
54. Tolmie, *Persuading the Galatians*, 24–27.
55. Ibid., 247.
56. This is eloquently put by Kenneth Burke in *Rhetoric*, 41: "the use of words by human agents to *form attitudes* or to *induce actions* in other agents" (emphasis added). Richards, in *Rhetoric*, 13, expands this notion by declaring that "rhetoric is more than a taxonomy of linguistic devices and persuasive strategies; it is also a process of argument, a way of thinking which understands that all positions are arguable."
57. Tolmie, *Persuading the Galatians*, 27–29.

1. Identify the dominant rhetorical strategy of a section. This involves answering two primary questions:

    - How can one describe the author's primary rhetorical objective in the particular section?
    - How does the author set about achieving this objective?

The answers to the above questions enable one to describe the dominant rhetorical strategy of the section, which is then expressed in a single sentence.

2. Create a detailed analysis of the author's rhetorical strategy in a particular section. While flexibility is maintained with regard to the approach for each section, a general rather than a fixed methodological approach is followed to achieve a description of the *main characteristics* of the author's strategy in a particular section, which may involve describing:

    - *The type of argument* or the nature of a specific argument, or
    - *The way in which an author argues* or employs a process of argumentation to achieve a particular rhetorical objective.

3. Where deemed necessary, identify the "supportive" rhetorical strategies important for the overall argument of a section or for the entire discourse. Strategies that cannot be directly related to the dominant rhetorical objective fall into this category. In the present analysis, I have not deemed it necessary to identify any "supportive" strategies; hence, this terminology will not be utilized.

4. Identify the rhetorical techniques within a section. These involve the ways in which an author enhances the effectiveness of his or her communication, e.g., metaphor, rhetorical questions, paronomasia (word play), the way sentences are constructed, and chiasmus.

5. Describe the organization of the argument in the letter as a whole.

Tolmie's *text-centered rhetorical criticism*[58] or *minimal theory framework* is a pristine specimen of rhetorical critical innovation along with that of Classen and indicates a growing trend away from utilizing

---

58. At least one other researcher has experimented with the method. See also Snyman, "Philippians."

classical rhetoric.⁵⁹ I apply the general tenets of this methodology and specifically appreciate the principle of textual priority or integrity that appears to motivate or undergird it. Thus, the text rather than the ancient rhetorical model becomes the "starting point." In this way, what Olbricht calls "the text and its power,"⁶⁰ moves to the foreground. However, neither "text-centered" nor "minimal theory framework" might be the best descriptors for the method. Despite the name of the latter descriptor, there is substantial theory embedded in the methodology.⁶¹ Thus, it presupposes knowledge of classical rhetorical theory and form criticism.⁶² Also, while Tolmie acknowledges the ambiguity associated with the term *rhetoric*, he nevertheless, after qualification, opts to use it.⁶³

This incredibly valuable method could benefit from some well-intentioned modifications. In a future publication, I will set out a systemization thereof. At this juncture, I propose the rationale for a more suitable name change. The basic premise is the centrality of *persuasive intent* on the part of the author of an epistle. The second premise is *textual sufficiency* for analyzing and reconstructing persuasive intent. Hence, the name that I attribute to this method is *text-generated persuasion analysis*. The ground rules having been established, it is time to proceed with the analysis of Titus.

---

59. See also Welch, *Contemporary*, for a defense of classical rhetoric. She claims defiantly that "[c]lassical rhetoric has never disappeared" then asks a question, answered in the rest of her book: "Why will it not go away?" See also, Anderson, *Rhetorical Theory*, 26, and Du Toit, "Alienation," 280, on the place and value of ancient rhetorical theory.

60. Olbricht, "Rhetorical Criticism," 26; see also Meynet, *Rhetorical Analysis*, 177, who believes in letting the text "speak for itself," or put differently, to "trust in the text and in its own internal logic" instead of contorting it to fit into the rigors of a preexistent model.

61. Tolmie has extensive experience spanning more than twenty years in the discipline; see the preface to *Persuading the Galatians*, which shows that his understanding of his own system is virtually intuitive. The theoretical framework of this innovative method requires refinement and systematization. This will enhance its user-friendliness and expose it to the broader academic playing field.

62. E.g., form critically, there is the assumption of familiarity with the epistolary genre. Classic rhetorically, there has to be knowledge of the epistolary structure to appreciate that an "adaptation" of the salutation occurred.

63. Tolmie, *Persuading the Galatians*, 1.

2

Titus 1:1–4

Adapting the Salutation to Emphasize the Divine Basis of Legitimate Ministry

THE SALUTATION IS ONE of five categories of a typical Pauline letter. In it, Paul would normally identify himself as the sender, specify the recipient(s), and continue with a greeting, thanksgiving, or a prayer.[1] Titus demonstrates that Paul could deviate from his normal pattern with relative ease, since this letter, for example, does not contain a thanksgiving section. Scholars recognize the unusual nature of this salutation, and in this regard, Collins observes that "salutations were much more than an envelope for a letter: they too had a rhetorical function," which he argues involved getting the attention of the audience and rehearsing facts upon which the audience and the speaker agreed.[2] He continues by observing that salutations were similar to the first century rhetorical categories of *exordium* and *narratio*. In the case of the Letter to Titus, the dominant rhetorical objective of the salutation is *to emphasize the divine basis of legitimate ministry*. The analysis of this section will show that multifaceted objectives lie behind Paul's digression from his usual pattern.

Emphasizing the Legitimacy of Paul's Ministry

This letter opens in a most unique manner. Paul situates his modified self-identification within the realm of the divine (Παῦλος δοῦλος θεοῦ,

---

1. McRay, *Paul*, 265, 267; Harvey, *Listening*, 18; Tolmie, *Persuading the Galatians*, 31.
2. Collins, "Epistle to Titus," 59.

ἀπόστολος δὲ Ἰησοῦ Χριστοῦ). The two anarthrous nouns, δοῦλος and ἀπόστολος, immediately link Paul to God and Jesus Christ; first as a servant of the former, next, as an apostle of the latter. This sentence, from the outset, communicates the author's belief in the equality of God and Jesus Christ, which is reiterated in verse 4. Additionally, there is a sense in which Paul stresses the dual authorization of his ministry by locating it with God and Jesus Christ. While his ministry derives its authority from God and Jesus Christ, it remains focused on a single entity, namely the elect of God (ἐκλεκτῶν θεοῦ).

Later in the sentence, Paul again emphasizes this notion of divine sanction of his ministry. In 1:3, he declares that he has been entrusted (ἐπιστεύθην) with a message. The emphatic use of the personal pronoun ἐγώ is unequivocal. Paul continues to accentuate the divine authorization of his ministry by stressing that he is serving according to the command of God (κατ' ἐπιταγὴν τοῦ . . . θεοῦ). Effectively, he is informing his audience why they should listen to him. The intent seems to be to convey the notion that only those who serve God and Jesus Christ can serve the church or advance the faith and knowledge of the church, for the purpose of godliness (πίστιν . . . καὶ ἐπίγνωσιν . . . κατ' εὐσέβειαν).

Coming through loud and clear is the fact that qualified or legitimized service in the church is an absolute necessity. Paul seems to communicate the notion that he did not simply wake up one day and decide that serving the church would be a noble vocation. No. He was entrusted, commanded (ἐπιταγή). He was serving God. He was sent by Jesus Christ. Thus, divine authorization or a theological motivation for legitimate ministry seems to be a central feature of this section.

It remains to be asked, why Paul is so emphatic about the authorization of his ministry? A reasonable conjecture can be presented. He appears, at this early stage, to address and counter a tendency among Cretan believers to accept or tolerate unqualified teachers. According to him, this is an untenable situation because the spiritual progress, namely, faith and knowledge, of a church, depends upon the quality of the leadership. Paul furthermore establishes himself as the supreme example of an authorized servant—one who has the right to speak to the church. However, unlike the situation envisioned in the Letter to the Galatians, here it is clear that it is not Paul's authority or credibility that is under attack. He is not writing to defend his ministry. Instead, he writes to set himself up as an example of legitimized ministry; one that has the right to address the church.

Specifying the Nature of Legitimate Teaching

References of a Doctrinal Nature

Paul's ministry is directed toward the faith and knowledge (κατὰ πίστιν . . . καὶ ἐπίγνωσιν) of the church or the elect of God (ἐκλεκτῶν θεοῦ). Thus, these two specific areas comprise the realm of legitimate ministry. It is a very specific knowledge that is the focus of attention, namely knowledge of "*the* truth" (ἀληθείας τῆς). Through an intricate series of prepositional phrases, Paul develops the twin concepts of faith and knowledge to their ethical conclusion. The preposition κατά features prominently in this opening section: κατὰ πίστιν ἐκλεκτῶν (1:1), κατ' εὐσέβειαν (1:1), κατ' ἐπιταγήν (1:3), and κατὰ κοινὴν πίστιν (1:4). According to Wallace, one of the basic functions of κατά with the accusative is to indicate standard, in which instance it is then translated as "in accordance with" or "corresponding to."[3] However, in the first instance above, the preposition is best understood to indicate the purpose of Paul's service and apostleship.[4] Thus, his ministry is "for the purpose of (the) faith," to further the faith,[5] "for (the) faith,"[6] or "in the interest of faith."[7] The repetition of the preposition, in this section, serves as a rhetorical technique that adds to the cohesiveness of this section. Interestingly, the unusual repetition of this preposition is located rather strategically throughout this section, forming what could be seen as an *inclusio*:

a. κατὰ πίστιν (1:1)

b. κατ' εὐσέβειαν (1:1)

c. κατ' ἐπιταγὴν (1:3)

d. κατὰ (κοινὴν) πίστιν (1:4)

While some take a different view, the second instance of the preposition also indicates purpose. This time it is not related to Paul but rather to

---

3. Wallace, *Greek Grammar*, 377.
4. Bernard, *Epistles*, 155.
5. Knight, *Pastoral Epistles*, 283.
6. Mounce, *Pastoral Epistles*, 379; Quinn, *Letter to Titus*, 62.
7. Hendriksen, *Timothy and Titus*, 340.

faith and knowledge. Faith and knowledge have as their goal or outcome the godliness of the elect. Faith is emphasized through the repetition of the word πίστις (1:1, 4) as well as through paronomasia of the same word group: πίστις (1:1, 4) and πιστεύω (1:3) in this section: godliness in turn, is motivated by, or premised upon, the hope of eternal life (1:2). Paul is meticulous in defining knowledge. He uses the genitive to limit the meaning to "knowledge of the truth" (ἐπίγνωσιν ἀληθεάς τῆς). Here, "the truth," modified by the article, constitutes the gospel, in particular that body of objective truth.

The faith of God's elect, along with knowledge, truth, and godliness specify the parameters of legitimate ministry. In the first place, there is a specific group or category of people that are related to God in a particular manner. God elected them. Thus, they are God's. Next, the legitimate ministry relates to a specific body of truth, namely ἀληθείας τῆς κατ' εὐσεβειαν. The purpose of the apostolic ministry is to bring about a behavioral or ethical adjustment (εὐσέβεια) in view of the life to come.

The certainty of this hope is guaranteed. Paul bases his argument upon the *integrity of the divine* or the reliability of God, specifying that God's ethical character is ἀψευδής. He continues to emphasize that this hope was never dependent upon humanity. God promised it, God brought it about. Through the use of temporal references, namely, πρὸ χρόνων αἰωνίων (1:2) and καιροῖς ἰδίοις (1:3), Paul ensures that no credit accrues at any stage to any human being. His argument is based on *divine authorization* and *divine initiation*. The hope of eternal life was manifested in the word of God (τόν λόγον αὐτοῦ). Verse 3 reiterates the divine authorization of the apostle's ministry, in which he strips even himself from any credit for the proclamation (κηρύγμα). Thus, the messenger as well as the content of the message must be divinely authorized.

References to God

There are five references to God in this section. This constitutes a high-occurrence ratio for a single noun in such a small section. When two appearances in the *inclusio* framing this section are temporarily set aside, the remaining instances are very revealing. The *inclusio* referred to previously is the repetition of the nouns *God* and *Jesus Christ* in verses 1 and 4.

The first reference pertains to the church as ἐκλεκτοί θεοῦ. It is juxtaposed with δοῦλος θεοῦ in verse 1. Thus, Paul's service and apostleship are directed toward a particular group, namely the elect of God. The kind of ministry presented here is specified as a divinely sanctioned ministry, directed toward a group, whose origins the apostle locates in the divine.

Next, God's character is accentuated by the expression ὁ ἀψευδὴς θεός (1:2). This description occurs in the context of the promise that God made. Thus, the divine character or ethic is used to highlight the reliability of the divine promise. What God has promised has been fulfilled. The affirmation of the divine character furthermore implies the imposition of a norm. If God cannot lie, then God's servant cannot either, or at least would be expected to be honest.

The third reference occurs in 1:3 where God is referred to as Savior (σωτήρ). Thus, we are dealing here with the divine origin of salvation. In the next verse, the same description is applied to Jesus Christ.

This section is suffused with the role of the divine. The elect have their origin in God. The promise made before the ages was fulfilled because of the character of God. The reason there is an elect and the reason for the ethic required of the elect is because God is also the one who saved them. Thus, a central theme in this first section is the notion of the divine. It takes away all credit from humanity and places the focus on the central and dominating character of God.

References to Jesus Christ

Verses 1–4 contain two references to Jesus Christ. The first reference in 1:1 is repeated, but reversed in 1:4. These references appear to accentuate the divinity of Jesus Christ, who, in both instances, is presented as equal to God. In the first instance, the name of Jesus is mentioned in the context of ministry, specifically the apostolic office. In the next instance, it is mentioned in the context of salvation. Interestingly, though, God is also mentioned in both of these contexts.

In 1:1, Paul relates his ministry first to God and next, as apostle, to Jesus Christ. The first reference to Jesus Christ is in a coordinate relationship with the noun θεός. Some commentators interpret the conjunction δέ in a connective sense as "and." However, it can also be interpreted in a contrastive or adversative sense as "yet" or "but." The apostle thus introduces himself by laying the foundation for his authority to address Titus and the church. On the one hand, he is only a bond servant of God. However, on the other hand, his office is that of an apostle, authorized by Jesus Christ.

In 1:4, he refers to Jesus Christ as σωτήρ ἡμῶν. This is the exact designation used in the preceding verse to refer to God. Thus, God and Jesus Christ are introduced as co-saviors to whom the salvific activity is attributed. This is accentuated through the rhetorical technique, chiasmus:

| A—τοῦ σωτῆρος | B—ἡμῶν θεοῦ (1:3) |
| B*—Χριστοῦ Ἰησοῦ | A*—τοῦ σωτῆρος ἡμῶν (1:4) |

Another striking feature of this passage is the way in which it begins and ends. Verse 1 starts with θεοῦ . . . Ἰησοῦ Χριστοῦ, while verse four ends with θεοῦ . . . Χριστοῦ Ἰησοῦ. Except for the reversal of Jesus Christ to Christ Jesus, the order is essentially identical. This is known as an *inclusio*. Why did the apostle deem it necessary to accentuate the divinity of Jesus in this manner, namely by equating him with God? Why is he so painstakingly meticulous to ensure that the recipient(s) are properly orientated toward Jesus Christ? Could it be that he was perhaps preempting erroneous notions about the divinity of Christ? Was part of the erroneous doctrine that was perpetuated by the false teachers related to an incomplete or compromised Christology? An answer in the affirmative would not seem unreasonable in this regard.

Emphasizing the Legitimacy of the Ministry of Titus

Whereas Paul's authority is derived from God, the legitimization of the ministry of Titus comes from the apostle. Titus is referred to by name (1:4). This designation is expanded through the use of kinship language as exemplified in the expression γνησίῳ τέκνον. In return, the kinship is made emphatic by the assonance of the ω sound when referring to Titus as Τίτῳ γνησίῳ τέκνῳ. Furthermore, the language serves to bestow honor upon Titus before the congregation. This is an early occurrence of the rhetorical technique I call *honorific referencing* or *classification*.

Toward the end of the salutation, the transcendent quality of the language yields to the language of imminence, activated through familial or relational referents. Tenderness is introduced by referring to Titus as Paul's child and later claiming God as Father (1:4). The reference to God as "Father" levels the proverbial playing fields, since it makes God the source of Paul as well as of Titus. The ἐκλεκτοί θεοῦ are from a salvific perspective the offspring of the divine, but so are Paul and Titus. Titus's ministry at Crete is couched in the language of a son who stands in the service of his father, conjuring up images of loyalty and trustworthiness. This choice of language constitutes an argument of authorization based on paternal or parental validation. Furthermore, it has the effect of confirming to the audience (including the illegitimate teachers) that Titus is acting as an authorized representative of the apostle.

Other rhetorical techniques used in this section include the unusual repetition of the preposition κατά, *inclusio*, chiasmus, paronomasia, *honorific referencing* or *classification*, and repetition of the πίστις word group.

CONCLUSION

In this section, Paul's dominant rhetorical strategy has been *to adapt the salutation to emphasize the divine basis of legitimate ministry*. He starts by establishing his own authority and concludes by endorsing the ministry of Titus by apostolic and divine authorization. His reason for doing this is not because he is under attack, but rather because he wants to highlight the notion of legitimate ministry. It remains to be asked, why does the apostle adopt this specific approach?

The salutation contains information that would be redundant if primarily addressed to someone who knew the apostle as well as Titus. Instead, the very nature of the address, the loftiness of the theology and the inflexible insistence upon highlighting the role of the divine suggests that Paul had a wider audience in mind. Some scholars conclude this based on the plural pronoun reference in 3:15, but a larger audience is already discernible in the salutation as suggested by the use of *inclusive language*. In 1:3, Paul refers to God as ὁ σωτήρ ἡμῶν. Are we expected to believe that the apostle is referring here exclusively to himself and Titus? In other words, is the apostle suggesting that God is only the Savior of the two of them? Would someone like Titus need to be persuaded about Paul's authority? Or would he need to be taught about the content of legitimate teaching? The answer is obvious. Paul is addressing the church at Crete. The reference to θεός πατέρ is another example of the rhetorical technique of *inclusive language* that cannot simply be applicable to the apostle and his delegate. It is interesting to note the expansion or development with reference to God. In 1:1 Paul is δοῦλος θεοῦ, and the church is ἐκλεκτῶν θεοῦ. The next description that follows describes God as ὁ ἀψευδὴς θεός. Beyond this point, God is mentioned in the context of a plural modifier as σωτήρ ἡμῶν and in a paternal nuance as θεός πατέρ. God is therefore the key protagonist, the leading actor in this unfolding drama of salvation.

3

Titus 1:5–9

Outlining the Criteria for Legitimate Local Leadership

Having established himself as a legitimate minister of the church, the apostle concludes the salutation by introducing and affirming Titus as his representative. From verse 5 onward, he develops the concept of legitimate ministry by embarking upon his dominant rhetorical objective, namely, outlining the criteria for legitimate local congregational leadership. Conspicuously missing at this point is the characteristic thanksgiving section.[1] A possible reason for this absence could be that there was nothing to give thanks for, which in turn, could confirm scholarly conjecture that the congregation was relatively young and had been established fairly recently. Since there is nothing to give thanks for, Paul unceremoniously launches into his topic with great eagerness.

Paul employs arguments based on authority, namely apostolic authority, in order to firstly justify Titus's presence on the island of Crete and secondly to underscore his authority among the Cretan believers. In verse 5, Paul declares that he left Titus in Crete (ἀπέλιπον σε ἐν Κρήτῃ). Now, in all probability, Titus knew that Paul had left him in Crete. He would also have understood or at least had some idea, before his arrival, of the nature of his assignment. So why would Paul now write in this manner? The answer lies in our understanding of who the recipients of the letter are. The language suggests that Titus cannot be the only recipient. It has to include a wider audience, in whose presence, in all

---

1. Classen, *Rhetorical Criticism*, 51.

probability, this letter would have been read publically. Verse 5 answers questions like, "What are you doing here in Crete?" or, "By whose authority are you implementing these procedures?" or, "Who gave you command over us?" These kinds of questions are answered by the details provided in verse 5. The concluding clause provides the authorization for Titus to fulfill his mandate. In this regard, the use of the first person personal pronoun (ἐγώ) together with the verb in the first-person singular (διεταξάμην) is deliberately emphatic. Paul stresses that *he* is the one who has directed Titus. Interestingly, the tense of the verb, namely aorist middle, points to a time prior to that when Titus would have received this letter. These are therefore not new directives. Although the verb διατάσσω (1:5) is weaker in import than the noun ἐπιταγή in 1:3, it functions in the same way as the noun. This is an instance of the use of synonyms for emphasis, which facilitates intrasectional cohesion. Paul's authority derives directly from God while that of Titus comes indirectly from the apostolic directive. In other words, there is a hierarchy of command where authority flows from the divine through the apostle to Titus and ultimately to the local leaders. However, Paul's choice of language indicates that he does not consider his authority to appoint a leader, in this instance, to be equal with that of God. Hence, he *directs* (διατάσσω) Titus, but God *commanded* (κατ' ἐπιταγήν) Paul. It remains to be asked why Paul would write in such a roundabout manner. The apostle is perhaps adopting an anticipatory stance in view of some opposition against the presence of Titus. Already, we find in Crete teachers who were "upsetting whole households" (1:11). Titus's presence would not be amicably received within such a context. The teachers, it seems, held at least some degree of sway among the congregations. The difference between them and Titus is a significant one, as the salutation and verse 5 indicate: Titus represents legitimate leadership, while those in Crete are illegitimate. At a different level, the apostle is educating the Cretan believers about legitimate church leadership. He is about to develop his lesson, by providing objective criteria to ensure that the believers would be able to distinguish legitimate teachers from those who presume to be teachers. By so doing, he is laying a foundation for the appointment of leaders in the future, i.e., those who will be appointed in the absence of apostles and apostolic delegates.

The basis upon which these other teachers attained a position of influence over the church is not clear. There seems to have been an indiscriminate tolerance, if not acceptance, by the church of these persons as well as of their teachings. Paul's purpose in this section, therefore, appears to be providing objective evaluation criteria in order to establish legitimate or authorized leadership in the Cretan church.

In the salutation, Paul alluded to the purpose of legitimate ministry, namely the maintenance of the character of God's people as ἐκλεκτοί θεοῦ. Starting with himself, Paul showed that even he had to comply with certain criteria through the use of the nouns δοῦλος and ἀπόστολος.

Now, in verses 6–9, he is developing the notion that serving the church of God is not the domain of individual preferment. There are conditions to be met. Since compliance criteria are acceptable in secular business, how much more among the ἐκλεκτοί θεοῦ? Those who serve in the church ought to serve the interests of God rather than their own interests. The overseer is after all called a θεοῦ οἰκόνομος (1:7). Note how Paul, in his capacity as the δοῦλος θεοῦ (1:1) serving the ἐκλεκτοί θεοῦ (1:1), now prescribes the criteria for those whom he refers to as the θεοῦ οἰκονόμοι (1:7). The consistent pattern emerging from these few verses is one that makes all who serve in the church accountable to God (θεός).

Paul's objective is clear, namely to provide observable or measurable criteria by which to ensure legitimate leadership in the church. Mappes suggests that the qualifications for elders serve as a polemic against the false teachers.[2] Some, like Dibelius and Conzelmann have pointed out the resemblance between the lists in the Pastorals with first-century character codes.[3] The stipulated criteria would also serve to explain or defend Titus's selection of some and not others. In other words, these standards effectively clear Titus's actions from potential charges of arbitrariness or subjectivity. More important, though, is the rhetorical significance of the list. In a recent work, Tolmie categorized similar lists in Galatians as constituting "shared knowledge."[4] The qualities cited in verses 6–9 are not exclusive to the Christian context. Extrabiblical evidence corroborates that such norms were considered reasonable by the broader society of first-century Hellenistic culture.[5] If secular Cretan society therefore endorsed these standards, it would be very hard to defend the behavioral conduct of leaders that did not comply with these

2. Mappes, "Moral Virtues," 214.
3. Dibelius and Conzelmann, *Pastoral Epistles*, 158.
4. Tolmie, *Persuading the Galatians*, 216, 217.
5. Dibelius and Conzelmann, *Pastoral Epistles*, 158.

shared or common standards. Rhetorically, this has the positive effect of rendering Paul's prescriptions reasonable, since his audience would be familiar with these criteria. Negatively, it would be almost impossible to justify tolerating anyone whose actions contradict the societal norm.

Those responsible to minister to the ἐκλεκτοί θεοῦ ought to be examples of the power of the truth (1:1). Their lives and conduct must give evidence of the reliability of the promises of God. The first to manifest εὐσέβεια are the leaders. Faith in God, or the εὐσέβεια ἐπ' ἐλπίδι ζωῆς αἰωνίου (1:1, 2), is neither cerebral nor merely confessional (cf. 1:16). Instead, it is practical and observable. Scholars who overeagerly emphasize the similarities that these character requirements share with secular lists downplay the powerful statement made here concerning the gospel or *the truth* (1:1). Those appointed become the direct antitheses of the illegitimate teachers. That men of this caliber can even be found in such a context is an incredible testimony to the power of God's word. In other words, the manifestation of the divine promise is not an abstract event. It changes lives and produces the kind of men described in 1:6–9.

To whom is this written? Both Titus and the Cretans are the intended audience of these lists. However, Titus is only a secondary recipient. He, perhaps, needs only a reminder. The primary recipients are the Cretans. The sheer detail provided in this section suggests a didactic function. There can be no mistaking that anyone hearing the content of this letter would leave with an almost graphic image of the legitimate leader. Doubtless, there would be those followers of the illegitimate teachers who would now be empowered with an objective standard by which to measure their teachers to whose influence they have fallen victim (1:11).

According to Johnson, the catalogue of vices and virtues in 1:6–9 evinces several instances of unique vocabulary.[6] It contains three words unique to the New Testament (ἐπιδιορθόω, φιλάγαθος, ἐγρατής) and fifteen Pauline *hapax legomena*. Of the latter, nine appear in the rest of the Pastorals (ἀπολείπω, φιλόξενος, πάροιμος, πλήκτης, αἰσχροκερδῆς, σώφρον, πρεσβυτέρος, ὅσιος, ὑγιαίνω) while six never occur in the Pauline corpus (Κρήτη, λείπω, κατηγορία, ἀνυπότακτος, αὐθάδης, ὀργίλος). Incidentally, Johnson maintains that the variation in vocabulary can be explained by the variation in subject matter.[7] It is preferable to interpret these *hapaxes* as context-specific vocabulary. This is based on the assumption that in

6. Johnson, *Paul's Delegates*, 220.
7. Ibid., 221.

the mind of the author, the recipients would have been familiar with the vocabulary. The anaphoric μη is another device employed to highlight the five vices in 1:7. Anaphora is also used in two words in the virtue list. They occur in 1:8, namely φιλόξενος and φιλάγαθος. Both adjectives are compound nouns prefixed by the noun φιλός. These rhetorical techniques highlight the arenas of the elder overseer's personal life under observation, namely marriage, family life, and personality or attitudinal behavior. Moreover, the prefix φιλός emphasizes the attitude of love that should characterize the elder overseer.

The cohesion between this section and the salutation is effected through the repetition of specific vocabulary. For example, the noun πίστις recurs several times in the space of a few verses: κατὰ πίστιν ἐκλεκτῶν θεοῦ (1:1), κατὰ κοινὴν πίστιν (1:4), ἀντεχόμενον τοῦ ... πιστοῦ λόγου (1:9). Additionally, the word λόγος (1:3) is repeated in verse 9.

Paul also uses transitional devices to introduce the different sections. In 1:4, he introduced Titus and proceeded to address him in verse 5. Now, in 1:9, he introduces the opposition or the illegitimate teachers as οἱ ἀντιλέγοντες. What is it that they contradict or oppose? It must be the teaching, here made conspicuous by the interchangeable use of the nouns διδαχή and διδασκαλία, respectively, within the same sentence: κατὰ τὴν διδαχὴν and ἐν τῇ διδασκαλίᾳ τῇ ὑγιαινούσῃ. The conditions for elders culminate in verse 9 with the criterion to "hold to the faithful word": ἀντεχόμενον τοῦ κατὰ τὴν διδαχὴν πιστοῦ λόγου. Thus, over and above the character requirements, the relationship of the individual elder to the word is paramount. The idea of "the word" was introduced in the salutation, 1:3. There it was the divine word that was "manifested" (ἐφανέρωσεν δὲ καιροῖς ἰδίοις τὸν λόγον αὐτοῦ). According to 1:9, the elder must cling to the "faithful word." This description would call to mind the earlier reference in 1:3. The authority of the elder derives directly from the word, which enables him to do two things, namely "to exhort" (παρακαλεῖν) and "to refute" or "convince" (ἐλέγχειν). It is at this point that the issue of opposition is introduced. The distinguishing factor between legitimacy and illegitimacy hinges on the relationship of the opposing parties to the manifested word. The antithesis between the two groups is highlighted through the intentional play on the two participles used to refer to them: ἀντεχόμενοι and ἀντίλεγοντες. Both are prefixed by the preposition ἀντί, generally meaning "against."[8] The first

---

8. Zodhiates, *Dictionary*, s.v. "ἀντί."

word connotes a positive stance, the second a negative action. Paul, in this way, introduces the next step in his strategy, namely, the vilification of the opposition. In this transitional sentence, the apostle juxtaposes their negative behavior with the positive behavior of the overseer. The opposition is thus introduced here as "the ones who speak against." They contradict the action of the overseer who "holds against" or "clings to." The rhetorical objective of this brilliant use of a prefix is to launch his denigration of the opposition.

CONCLUSION

In this section, the dominant rhetorical objective is *to outline criteria for the establishment of legitimate local leadership in the church*. His arguments are primarily based on authority, particularly apostolic authority. Thus, Titus's presence and jurisdiction are authorized by apostolic directive. The detailed explanations, in the form of a catalogue of vices and virtues, are examples of the rhetorical technique called *shared knowledge*. Its use suggests that this section is primarily targeted at the congregation. It addresses Titus only secondarily. The leader must be blameless in his family life as well as in his behavior. In other words, his life must bear testimony to the fact that he has embraced the Christian doctrine. Through the rhetorical technique of repetition, Paul links this section to the preceding salutation, developing certain notions like faith and the primacy of the word. Another rhetorical technique, anaphora, is used to draw attention to the vices and virtues related to the elder overseers and concludes the catalogue by specifying the most important qualification, namely the ability to teach the word. In this regard, the elder overseers are made responsible for exhortation and refutation.

Also present on the island are "those who contradict" and their followers. Paul uses the list of virtues and vices to educate the congregation regarding legitimate and illegitimate leadership. The list also represents shared knowledge, which constitutes an irrefutable argument in favor of the validity of the requirements for legitimate leadership. Another rhetorical technique used in this section is that of synonyms.

This section concludes with the legitimate leaders being pitched against the illegitimate ones. Furthermore, the closing sentence (1:9) serves as a transitional device that introduces the vilification of the illegitimate leaders. In the following section, the disparagement of the opposition takes on a more fully developed form. We now have a clear picture of the legitimate leaders. Next, there follows an introduction to the problem of illegitimate leaders.

4

Titus 1:10–16

Discrediting the Illegitimate Teachers

IN VERSE 6 AND following, Paul focuses his audience's attention upon the "opposition," whom he will eventually expose as being presumptive teachers (1:11). Through the use of a transitional sentence, Paul introduces them in the latter part of verse 9 as τοὺς ἀντιλέγοντας. We first encounter them in the context of a conflict situation, at the receiving end of the ministry of the elders, who must reprove (ἐλέγχειν) them. This sentence introduces an us/them dichotomy at the front end of this letter (1:9) that is expanded in the subsequent verses (1:10–16). The dominant rhetorical objective in this section is to discredit the illegitimate teachers primarily by magnifying their illegitimacy. The rhetorical technique employed involves the vilification of the illegitimate teachers.

Vilification

Vilification is a persuasive technique used by an author or speaker to present opposing parties or the parties' viewpoints in a negative light, by magnifying some aspects of character or propositional weakness, with a view to influence audience members to disassociate themselves from the opposition or the viewpoint and endorse the position of the speaker or writer. Du Toit correctly considers vilification to have been a "widespread convention . . . obtained throughout the Mediterranean world."[1] Botha calls it "invective," because it aimed to "dispose hearers

---

1. Du Toit, "Vilification," 404. See also Dio Chrysostom *Discourses* 4.33, 4.37, 4.38, 11.4, 55.7, 70.10.

favourably to the speaker and to shame and humiliate the 'enemy.'"[2] One of the ways in which it was employed involved portraying the opposition as those who were perverting the true faith and who were negative influences on the faith of others.[3] Paul, in order to achieve his dominant rhetorical objective, makes extensive use of vilification to portray the opposition in a very negative light. The impact and overall domination of the technique in this section becomes obvious from the following list describing illegitimate teachers, who are:

1. insubordinate, empty talkers, deceivers (v. 10)
2. upsetting whole families (v. 11)
3. teaching for gain (v. 11)
4. teaching without the right to teach (v. 11)
5. liars / evil beasts / lazy gluttons (v. 12)
6. giving heed to Jewish myths (v. 14)
7. giving heed to the commands of men who reject the truth (v. 14)
8. corrupt and unbelieving (v. 15)
9. corrupt in mind and conscience (v. 15)
10. denying God by their deeds (v. 16)
11. detestable, disobedient, unfit for any good deed (v. 16)

Verse 10 immediately takes up and builds upon the hostility introduced in the latter part of verse 9. The apostle unleashes his verbal artillery upon the aberrant ones through a technique I call *emphatic clustering*. He groups together three words to launch his vilification campaign, namely ἀνυπότακτος, ματαιολόγος, and φρεναπάτης. This linguistic triplet, combined with the adjective πᾶς, intensifies the hostile sentiment that this section intends to create. It furthermore serves as justification for the apostolic directives that this correspondence conveys. Structurally, it cordons off this section and magnifies the denigration to follow.

The vilification procedure is facilitated by several additional techniques, such as *implicit contrasting*. That which is contrasted is not made obvious within a sentence. In other words, the author gives no linguistic clues that a contrast is being made, for example, by using the words "like"

---

2. Botha, "Verbal Art," 421; see also Boonzaaier, "Vilifikasie," 1276.
3. Du Toit, "Vilification," 409.

or "just as." Instead, the author provides the information in such a manner that the hearer or reader, almost intuitively, "sees" the glaring contrasts within the larger discourse unit. For example, the description of the opposition in this section is implicitly contrasted with the positive character requirements associated with the office of the overseer mentioned earlier. The negative attitude of the opposition toward the word (1:9) is made plausible by the pejorative description of the opposition's character, which manifests firstly as insubordination (ἀνυπότακτος). This noun was used earlier with reference to the children of elders (1:6). This is an example of repetition. The effect is to evoke strong disapproval from the congregation for childish behavior on the part of the opposition. Unruly behavior demands strong disciplinary retaliation.

The noun ματαιολόγος follows rapidly upon the first and is suggestive of the apostolic view of the aberrant teaching. Such teaching is vain, empty, and lacking substance. In fact, the false teachers are the personification of what they teach. They themselves are empty and vain. The final noun in this cluster, φρεναπάτης, describes the opposition as deceivers or impostors. In other words, they are unauthorized, their claims of authority are invalid, and hence they are unqualified to minister to the church. Implicit contrasting is also operative here. Thus, compared to everyone mentioned in the previous two sections, this group of impostors does not match the leadership profile. While the group may be substantial, the apostle appears to single out a Jewish faction within the larger group, through the adjectival phrase μάλιστα οἱ ἐκ τῆς περιτομῆς. Johnson suggests that this expression might refer to Gentile Cretans who have come to embrace Judaism through the influence of Jewish teachers.[4] If this is so, the resemblance to Galatians would be, in his words, "all the more striking."[5]

The effect upon the hearers is nothing short of riveting: if this is what the apostle says about these people, how dare some believers think amicably about them? At this very point, the congregants are forced to pick sides. The tone of the letter has been positive up to the first half of verse 9 as it mentions Paul, Titus, and the elders elect. It will, however, from here onward, become calculatedly negative.

Verse 11 offers additional justification for the severe treatment of this insubordinate faction. The reasoning relates firstly to the effect of their "ministry" among the believers. It is considered absolutely essen-

---

4. Johnson, *Paul's Delegates*, 227, 228.
5. Ibid., 228.

tial that these people be silenced or muzzled (ἐπιστομίζειν). Paul and the elders, however, are allowed to speak to or teach the believers (1:3, 9). The impact of the activities of the illegitimate teachers is that it subverts or overturns whole households (ὅιτινες ὅλους οἴκους ἀνατρέπουσιν).

The emphasis upon the negative effect on the family institution constitutes a further element in the vilification campaign against these people. The reference to households (οἴκοι) can either indicate house churches or families. Paul's vilification here is based on the family or kinship theme. This calls to mind related ideas that were introduced in the previous two sections. For example, in 1:4, God is referred to as θεός πατήρ while Titus is called Paul's τέκνον. The language is relational and familial. This kind of relationship is characterized by order and submission. The notion of family also features prominently in the criteria for elders. In 1:6, the elder is expected to demonstrate a positive influence upon his own family. All these disclose a positive attitude toward the family. The negative impact of the illegitimate teachers upon the family institution is thus exacerbated by the use of the kinship argument. This implicit contrast highlights an underlying argument suggestive of the importance of a stable family life in the ancient world. Whereas elder overseers must maintain a stable family life, the opposition threatens that stability, and they are vilified for it. The text, therefore, suggests that it is a severe form of vilification to accuse someone of threatening the family institution. Johnson points out that "[i]n the Greco-Roman world, insubordination or instability in the *oikos* was reason enough to condemn a religious movement."[6] Through a clever play on the word "house" or "household" (οἴκος), the apostle exploits the connotative value of the kinship argument with direct application to the church. In 1:7, he described the overseer as a "housekeeper" or "manager of God" (θεοῦ οἰκονόμος). The false teachers on the other hand, are subverting whole οἴκοι. Again, by implicit comparison to the elders, these impostors are shown to be illegitimate by highlighting the negative impact of their activities upon the church or individual families. They must be avoided because they prove to be outsiders who are predatory and harmful to families.

The next justification for the ruthless treatment of the impostors relates to the content of and the motivation for their teaching, which serves as a further basis for their vilification. Their illegitimacy relates to the content of their teaching, here described very unflatteringly as ἃ

---

6. Ibid., 235.

μὴ δεῖ (things not necessary). The insignificance of what they teach is expressed by the use of the relative pronoun (neuter) ἅ. The illegitimate teachers simply teach "things." Again, this is the opposite of what Paul and the elders teach. The selection of vocabulary heightens the polarity between the two groups. "Things" do not quite compare with "the truth," "the faithful word," "the teaching," and "healthy teaching" or "healthy doctrine" (1:1, 9). The readers must choose between being taught illegitimate "things" and legitimate "teaching."

The next two words, αἰσχροί κέρδοι, are further examples of paronomasia. It intentionally recalls a quality listed in the earlier catalogue of vices with reference to overseers, namely αἰσχροκερδής. If an overseer may not be αἰσχροκερδής, and since these false teachers are teaching for the sake of αἰσχροί κέρδοι, there is no way that the latter group can ever legitimately serve in God's οἶκος. They are disqualified. The language implies a warning to the believers. It is as if the apostle is saying, "Watch out. They are out to exploit you!" Clearly, he cannot be speaking to Titus. Those who stand to benefit from these caveats are the believers.

In verse 12, the apostle intensifies his strategy of vilifying the illegitimate teachers. His rhetorical strategy involves using *alienating* or *exclusive language* and making an *appeal to an external source of authority*. Paul's use of us/them language serves to alienate the believers from the illegitimate teachers. It also harnesses the notion of community and belonging. Here, he uses it negatively with reference to the illegitimate teachers. The repetition of the third-person plural form of the pronoun αὐτός (ἐξ αὐτῶν ἴδιος αὐτῶν προφήτης) emphasizes the notion of "them" and "us." More importantly, however, the repetition of the pronoun functions to corroborate the accusation that is expressed in the form of that infamous quote. Thus, here we have information about the false teachers from the proverbial horse's mouth—an inside story on their fundamental character.

Furthermore, Paul's rhetorical strategy involves an appeal to an external authority. The quote Κρῆτες ἀεὶ ψεῦσται κακὰ θηρία γαστέρες ἀργαί effectively points the attention of the hearers away from Paul. It is as if Paul is saying, "Don't be surprised. I'm not sucking these things out of my thumb. Here's what is said about them by someone who knows them. Here is what you know is true about them." The citation suggests a known source, insinuating that this is public knowledge. One could read into this citation a mild or implicit rebuke toward the congregation.

They should have known these things. However, if there is a rebuke, it is softened by the earlier use of the us/them language.

The quote demonstrates another instance of *emphatic clustering*. More specifically, we have here an example of *asyndetic emphatic clustering*. Together with verse 10, the quotation ties this section into a neat unit and maintains the vilification of the false teachers. The vocabulary employed is significant. Firstly, there is a play on the antonyms noticeable in the expressions Κρῆτες ἀεὶ ψεῦσται and ὁ ἀψευδὴς θεός (1:2). This is an instance of *implicit contrasting* where the character of the Cretans is juxtaposed with that of God. It furthermore establishes an argument based on example, and in this occurrence it is an irrefutable one, since the character of the opposition is presented as being diametrically opposed to the character of the divine. The next two descriptions, namely κακὰ θηρία and γαστέρες ἀργαί, have the effect of portraying the opposition as dehumanized by referring to them as beasts (θηρία) and lazy gluttons, or literally "idle stomachs." The rhetorical effect of this quotation is that it belittles the opposition in the eyes of the church. On its own, such vilification is rather damaging to any person's reputation. In the context of a local congregation, the relational consequences would be devastating.

In verse 13, the rhetorical strategy involves an *apostolic verification* of the saying regarding the Cretans' moral disposition. The use of the demonstrative pronoun αὕτη links this sentence to the citation. Here, Paul had the opportunity to limit the applicability of the earlier quotation; instead, he affirms the veracity of the Cretan poet's adage. There is a sense of irony associated with the combination of the quote and the apostolic affirmation: a Cretan poet brands Cretans as pathological liars, lazy bones, and gluttons. Scholars refer to this as the liar's paradox,[7] since it makes the statement a logical impossibility. The apostolic verification serves to corroborate the truth of the statement. Furthermore, we have repetition of the same word in the adjective ἀληθής. The corresponding noun ἀλήθεια was introduced in the salutation. Opponents would be hard pressed to refute the characterization, which is here intensified by the apostolic corroboration. A comparative view of the various units in chapter 1 discloses the development of a deliberate tension between truth and lies or liars: Paul's ministry is focused on the knowledge of ἀλήθεια (1:1). God is ἀψευδής (1:2). Next, the Cretans are ψεῦσται (1:12),

---

7. Mounce, *Pastoral Epistles*, 398.

while the statement is ἀληθής (1:13). Structurally, one could almost argue for an ABBA structure, but that is not the concern of this study.

The second part of verse 13 contains an instruction on the treatment of these false teachers. The second-person singular imperative of ἐλέγχω points to Titus as the primary addressee. This verb is repeated, having occurred earlier, where it applied to the overseer (1:9). Therefore, the responsibility to reprove the illegitimate teachers is shared by Titus and the overseers. Titus implicitly models to the others how an elder must exercise his ministry. The purpose clause, introduced by the conjunction ἵνα, serves to defend Paul's instructions against charges of malevolence. In spite of how bad they are, there is still hope for the impostors to become sound or healthy in the faith (ἵνα ὑγιαίνωσιν ἐν τῇ πίστει). The clause ὑγιαίνωσιν ἐν τῇ πίστει brings together in a single expression two words used in earlier sections, namely πίστις (1:1, 4, 6, 9) and the verb ὑγιαίνω. In the latter instance, it is the participial equivalent, namely ὑγιαινούσῃ (1:9), that is employed. Verse 13 suggests the possibility for transformation. Those who may have been led astray can become sound in the faith. The verse also expresses an implicit caution against the abuse of authority since the harsh treatment has a noble end, namely return to *the* faith. The article in this instance specifies the body of objective gospel teaching, synonymous to *the* truth (1:1).

Verse 14 describes the content of the false teaching that the impostors are embracing, thereby continuing the vilification. Through the use of two related verbs, the difference between legitimate and illegitimate teachers is intensified. While not directly synonymous, the two verbs are related, in that they share the verb ἔχω. Whereas the overseer must "cling to" (ἀντέχω) the faithful teaching, false teachers must *not* "pay attention" (μὴ προσέχω) to wrong doctrine. Several parallels are apparent in the description of the two groups. Firstly, both verbs share the primary root verb. Secondly, they are both in the present participial form. Thirdly, there is a definite contrast in regard to the content of the different teachings. In verse 14, the attention is apparently focused on Ἰουδαϊκοῖς μύθοις καὶ ἐντολαῖς ἀνθρώπων. In verse 9, it is τοῦ (κατὰ τὴν διδαχὴν) πιστοῦ λόγου. Note how the authorization of the illegitimate leaders derives from human authority (ἐντολαῖς ἀνθρώπων), while that of Paul originates directly from the divine (1:1–4). The ministry of Titus and the elders derives more indirectly from apostolic authorization (1:5–9). In this part of the verse, the object of vilification shifts temporarily from individuals to the doctrinal origin of the false teaching. False doctrine derives from humans and is authorized by humans. Sound doctrine derives from God and is authorized by God.

The next participial phrase, ἀποστρεφόμενοι τὴν ἀλήθειαν, refocuses the attention on those who are targets of the vilification campaign. Throughout this entire sentence, the comparisons are implicit. The illegitimate teachers have reneged "the truth" (τὴν ἀλήθειαν) while Paul's entire ministry is focused on ἐπίγνωσιν ἀληθείας τῆς κατ' εὐσέβειαν (1:1). This description in verse 14, of the opposition's relationship to the truth, constitutes the climax in the vilification of the opposition. Here is the fundamental difference between legitimate and illegitimate ministry, namely the latter's abandonment of the truth. Verses 13 and 14 are one sentence in Greek. It opens and closes with the word ἀληθεία, first as an adjective and then as a noun. The word chain is thus continued and serves to tie all the various units of this chapter together. The fact that God is ἀψευδής does not bode well for the false teachers and their relationship to (the) truth. The repetitive use of the truth/lie dichotomy highlights the illegitimacy of the false teachers and presents them in a diametrically opposite stance from the divine.

In verse 15, the apostle appears to zoom in on a key notion within the teaching of the false teachers, namely purity. He continues his vilification campaign by elaborating on the description of the teachings he introduced in verse 14. He accomplishes this through a technique described as antithetic presentation[8] or antithetic chiasmus,[9] which he combines with the assonance of the vowel α. Additionally, he uses the repetition of several key words to intensify his focus. The most obvious is the word καθαρός, which appears three times in this verse: πάντα καθαρὰ τοῖς καθαροῖς. τοῖς δὲ καὶ ἀπίστοις οὐδὲν καθαρόν. Next is the verb μεμίανω: μεμιαμμένοις ... μεμίανται. Whereas the noun πίστις was used earlier, the antonym ἄπιστος, which accentuates the contrasts between the different groups, is employed here. The author pursues his objective of vilifying the opponents, this time through contrasting the pure and the impure and by name calling: μεμιανμμένοις καὶ ἀπίστοις. A final technique is the parallelism in the structure AABA:

---

8. Tolmie, *Persuading the Galatians*, 33.
9. Quinn, *Letter to Titus*, 101.

A—πάντα καθαρὰ	A—τοῖς καθαροῖς
B—τοῖς δὲ μεμιαμμένοις καὶ ἀπίστοις	A*—οὐδὲν καθαρόν

The sentence introduces two groups: the pure versus the defiled and unbelieving. The sentence accentuates the futility of trying to attain purity when you are already defiled and unbelieving. The participle, μεμιανμμένος, is in the perfect tense and in the passive voice. It is translated as "those who have been defiled." The repetition of key vocabulary and concomitant parallel structure, plus the rhetorical technique of assonance, draw attention to what may have been a dominant feature of the aberrant teaching, namely ritual purity. Paul shoots this notion down by convincingly illustrating its futility. The second clause emphasizes the hopelessness of the efforts of the false teachers. Their defilement is not merely external but also internal: ἀλλὰ μεμίανται αὐτῶν καὶ ὁ νοῦς καὶ ἡ συνείδησις. In other words, they are totally defiled or utterly incapable of purity because their defilement extends to their minds (ὁ νοῦς) and their consciences (ἡ συνείδησις).

In verse 16, Paul's rhetorical strategy involves focusing on the ethical inconsistency of what the opponents are doing. They confess to know God (θεὸν ὁμολογοῦσιν εἰδεναι), but instead they deny God by their works (τοῖς δὲ ἔργοις ἀρνοῦνται). The contrast between "to know" and "they are denying" is obvious and intentional. The vilification comes in the form of an accusation that the false teachers are not serving God by their deeds, which is one of the fundamental tenets of Judaism and Christianity (e.g., Matt 7:21). The rhetorical effect of this approach is that it provides the hearers with additional criteria by which to evaluate these false teachers. This final criterion is the most damning of them all, since what the opponents believe about God finds ultimate expression in the way they conduct their lives. In their case, it amounts to a complete denial of the foundational teachings of Christianity and Judaism.

The verse concludes with an instance of polysyndetic *emphatic clustering* to complete this phase of vilification. The illegitimate teachers are βδελυκτοί (ὄντες) καὶ ἀπειθεῖς καὶ (πρὸς πᾶν ἔργον ἀγαθὸν) ἀδόκιμοι. The underlined words are all adjectives, masculine, nominative plural and are linked by conjunctions. Contrary to their appearance of purity, Paul describes the false teachers as ἀδόκιμος (abominable or detestable).

This interesting word is a New Testament *hapax legomenon*. It denotes that which is an abomination to God.[10] The word ἀπειθής denotes an unwillingness to be persuaded, a lack of belief, or disobedience.[11] The last word in the trilogy, ἀδόκιμος, means unapproved, unworthy, spurious, or worthless.[12] An ironic picture concludes this section. Those who profess to know God are considered an abomination to God. Having earlier referred to them as ἀπίστος, the apostle now uses the word ἀπειθής to express a similar thought but in stronger terms: they are beyond persuasion. The final word concludes the picture by accentuating the illegitimacy of these false teachers. The expression πᾶν ἔργον ἀγαθόν is a transitional device that refers to the next section and will be developed in the subsequent sections. The point is that such works cannot be expected from the false teachers and also not from those who subscribe to their teaching.

CONCLUSION

In this section, Paul's dominant rhetorical objective has been *to discredit the illegitimate leaders*. His primary rhetorical strategy involves vilifying of the opposition. Paul uses several techniques to facilitate his objective, which is reducing the opposition to a less than human state. Through the technique called *emphatic clustering*, he immediately and directly focuses the attention upon the impostors. This strategy magnifies the illegitimacy of the false teachers and provides justification for the apostolic vitriol that they receive in this section. The vilification is furthermore intensified through techniques like implicit contrasting. The negative qualities of the false teachers follow after the description of the qualifications for elder overseers. The proximity of the two pictures inevitably encourages the drawing of comparisons between the two groups. Paul goes beyond this to compare the false teachers with everyone else mentioned earlier, including God. This is made possible through the ingenious repetitions of synonyms and antonyms. For example, there is a deliberate play upon the truth/lie dichotomy made possible entirely by the repetition of words like "truth," "liars," and "unlying." The false teachers' lack of commitment

---

10. Zodhiates, *Dictionary*, s.v. "ἀδόκιμος"; Mounce, *Pastoral Epsitles*, 403.
11. Zodhiates, *Dictionary*, s.v. "ἀπειθής."
12. Ibid., s.v. "ἀδόκιμος."

to the truth is also highlighted through the repetition of the words "truth" and "the truth."

Alienating language, which involves the use of us/them language, is another technique employed in this section. This has the effect of isolating the false teachers as well as discouraging those believers who might be tempted to embrace aberrant teaching. In verse 12, Paul draws on external evidence to substantiate his position.

The use of examples is another one of several effective techniques employed in this section. Paul implicitly appeals to the example of the divine character when, through the use of the quote, he calls to mind verse 2 where God is described as one who cannot lie. In this quote, the Cretans are branded as liars. The parallel is glaring.

Paul eventually highlights an aspect of the false teaching that emphasizes purity. He exposes the futility of the teaching by using parallelism and concludes the section with another dose of emphatic clustering, just for emphasis. He also uses the rhetorical technique of assonance and introduces a new concept that he will develop in subsequent sections. This latter tendency is an example of a transitional device, something Paul has consistently done throughout this chapter.

5

Titus 2:1

Distinguishing Titus as a Minister of Sound Doctrine on the Basis of Apostolic Authorization

THIS SECTION FOLLOWS ON from the previous section where the author discredited the opposition through the rhetorical technique of vilification. Here, he is distinguishing Titus by commending him as a minister of sound doctrine with apostolic endorsement. Furthermore, the mandate of Titus is extended, in that he becomes responsible not only for the appointment of office bearers but also for the disbursement of sound doctrine to the believers. Titus is thus presented here as one who is qualified to teach the church, as opposed to the opposition (1:11).

The ministry of Titus is set apart from that of the false teachers in various ways. To achieve this task, the apostle uses several linguistic markers. First, there is the emphatic placement of the second-person singular personal pronoun σύ at the beginning of the sentence, together with the adversative conjunction δέ. While marking off the section as separate from the previous one, it also contrasts Titus's ministry by drawing attention to the apostolic imperative from which his ministry originates. If someone from Crete were to ask, "Why are you teaching these things to us?" Titus could answer, "The apostle Paul commanded me to." Next, Titus is commanded to "speak" (λαλέω). This is an interesting word choice. The false teachers were "teaching," διδάσκοντες (1:11). So, why does Paul not instruct Titus to "teach" (διδάσκω)? Why this change of vocabulary? Could it be that he wants to create some distance between Titus, here representing legitimate ministry and the false teachers who represent illegitimate ministry? Another option is that the close proximity to the remaining words in the sentence could have particularly distorted the meaning of διδασκαλία. Thus, he appears to be protecting the distinctive or technical sense of the word διδασκαλία. Alternatively, the variation of vocabulary might have been intended to avoid redundancy. This is an example of the rhetorical technique called paronomasia. A third marker is the use of the plural of the neuter relative pronoun, ἅ. This pronoun has an immediate correlation to the false teachers who, according to 1:11, teaches ἃ μὴ δεῖ. Rhythmically, with reference to meter, as well as aurally, with reference to assonance of the vowel α, and the diphthong ει, the relation between the words in their different contexts is undeniable. A hearer would immediately have picked up this similarity of sound and noticed the intended difference between what is said to Titus and what is said about the false teachers. Titus, unlike the false teachers, must speak "things suited to sound doctrine" (ἃ πρέπει τῇ ὑγιαινούσῃ διδασκαλίᾳ). Interestingly, the expression ἡ ὑγιαινούσῃ διδακαλία is here reversed, when compared to its first occurrence in 1:9. Furthermore, the first time these two words appear together is in the context of elder overseers, who must exhort (παρακαλέω). Now, Titus shares that responsibility as he must—speak (λάλεω) sound doctrine. Here, repetition is used to establish a positive association. The parallel between the verbs used is also unmistakable. Thus, Titus and the elder overseers are shown to be allies or associates, while the false teachers are portrayed as aliens. Purely through the choice of vocabulary, the apostle manages to distinguish the ministry of Titus and that of the elder overseers from that of the false teachers through the ingenious combination of the neuter article and an expression used earlier with reference to another set of validated ministers of the church: ἃ πρέπει τῇ ὑγιαινούσῃ διδασκαλίᾳ.

CONCLUSION

This section appears upon first inspection to be addressed to Titus. However, from a rhetorical angle, the manner in which the apostle ties this section to the preceding one suggests the existence of a wider audience. The rhetorical techniques used in this section include: paronomasia, meter, assonance, emphatic use of pronouns, and repetition. The opening sentence is directed *to distinguish Titus and what he does* as the apostolic delegate among the Cretan believers (1:5). This is the dominant rhetorical objective of this section. More important, though, is the fact that this verse also introduces the notion of healthy doctrine. In the next section (2:2–10), the concept of healthy doctrine will be developed in a comprehensive sense. The doctrine of the false teachers has been discredited in the previous section, and their profession of faith was shown to be nothing more than hot air because of their works (1:16). The false teachers were teaching "things not necessary" (1:11). Titus is distinguished as one entitled to teach something very specific, namely "things fitting for sound doctrine." In this section, Paul is simply validating his man.

6

Titus 2:2–10

Persuading the Cretans That Personal Conduct Compliant with Sound Doctrine Is Compulsory and Should Characterize All Believers

SOUND DOCTRINE IS GIVEN its fullest explanation in this section. In other words, it sets out to answer the question, what does sound doctrine *look* like? Paul correlates sound doctrine to the manifestation of right behavior. Earlier, in 1:10–16, right behavior was shown to be the key indicator of a genuine profession of faith in God (1:10–16). The false teachers by their deeds are denying God; conversely, believers by their deeds must confess their belief in God. Thus, the inseparable correspondence between deeds and sound doctrine is at the heart of Paul's rhetorical objective in this section. The author makes extensive use of the rhetorical method of implicit contrast to achieve this objective.

This section consistently highlights the distinction between sound and unsound doctrine. The objective seems to involve providing the Cretan believers with reasons why they should embrace sound doctrine as opposed to the "things" of the false teachers. The text suggests that part of what the apostle is countering in this letter is the tendency among Cretan Christians to tolerate unhealthy teachers. This weakness corroborates the theory of the relative newness of the church of Crete. It appears that they have not yet learned to discern between healthy and unhealthy teaching and were still in need of instruction in this regard. "Healthy doctrine" is never defined anywhere in this letter. This is probably explicable by the fact that Paul does not seem to treat it as a theoretical concept. Instead, sound doctrine appears to be manifested in practical, personal, and public conduct by all believers.

In 2:2–10, Paul delineates the behavior that will characterize obedience to healthy doctrine as manifested through the lives of different categories of believers. These groups seem to be arranged in a particular order and are clearly cordoned off from each other. In a footnote, Hendriksen draws attention to the rhetorical technique of a chiastic arrangement of the first four groups in this section:[1]

| A—older men (2:2) | B—older women (2:3) |
| B*— young women (2:4–5) | A*— young men (2:6) |

In verses 2–5, the author describes what behavior fitting for sound doctrine looks like for older men, older women, and younger women. This is followed by a purpose statement in the form of a ἵνα clause. In verses 6–7, he deals with the behavior of young men and of Titus, also followed by a ἵνα clause. The behavior of slaves is the final social category (2:9–10), and this too is followed by a ἵνα clause. The section thus comprises verses 2–10 and is further subdivided by three ἵνα clauses. The list is general and comprehensive.

The Behavior of Older Men

In verse 2, Paul directs attention to the conduct of older men in the congregation that will comply with sound doctrine. Here the noun πρεσβύτης (older man) appears, while earlier (1:5) its adjectival form, namely πρεσβύτερος, is used to refer to an officer of the church. The change in terminology suggests that this group is distinct from the leaders mentioned previously. Fee argues that the agreement between the characteristics for elder overseers and older men could be attributed to the fact that the former would be appointed from latter group.[2] Nevertheless, the language suggests that as members of the church, older men are expected to manifest observable behavior that confirms their standing as legitimate believers. Through the repetition of a similar word, the idea is communicated that there ought to be congruency between the behavior

---

1. Hendriksen, *Timothy and Titus*, 363.
2. Fee, *Titus*, 185.

of older men in the church and that of the leaders and vice versa. Thus, by their conduct, older men will confirm their allegiance to the teaching of those ministering to the church.

Next, the apostle employs *shared knowledge* as he lists the reasonable, expected conduct of those associated with the church. These constitute borrowings from secular society.[3] They must be νηφαλίοι σεμνοὶ σώφρονοι and ὑγιαίνοντες. The first and third adjectives communicate the idea of sensibleness, self-control, and sobriety. The word σεμνός refers to the dignified conduct of an elderly man in society and the church. Through the use of the adjective σώφρονος, this section is tied to the virtues associated with elder overseers (1:8) in the same way that Titus is associated with the elder overseers through the words ὑγιαινούσῃ διδασκαλίᾳ.

The participle ὑγιαίνοντες is the fourth quality in this list and is modified by three nouns that are all dative, feminine, and singular: τῇ πίστει τῇ ἀγάπῃ τῇ ὑπομονῇ. This is another instance of asyndetic *emphatic clustering*. Paul expects older men to manifest spiritual health or wholeness. In 1:13, Titus must rebuke false teachers that they may become "sound in the faith" (ἵνα ὑγιαίνωσιν ἐν τῇ πίστει). The same thing is expected of older men: ὑγιαίνοντες τῇ πίστει. This parallel expression signifies an instance of implicit *contrast* being made between the older men and the false teachers. The latter might become "sound" or "healthy" only after severe rebuke. The older men on the other hand, are "sound" or "healthy" as a result of legitimate teacher(s) who must "speak the proper things becoming sound doctrine," (λάλει ἃ πρέπει τῇ ὑγιαινούσῃ διδασκαλίᾳ). Older men must also be healthy in love and perseverance. The combination of these positive qualities appears to balance the citation with the three negative traits in 1:12. These qualities are therefore presented as commendable, made almost desirable. Thus, legitimate teaching is presented in a very positive light through the use of these rhetorical devices. The rhetorical objective is evidently to motivate the believers to manifest behavior that gives evidence of their compliance to ὑγιαινούσῃ διδασκαλίᾳ.

The participle of ὑγιαίνω is used in all three instances thus far, namely 1:9, 2:1, and 2:2. This is an instance of direct repetition. Sound doctrine ought to manifest as soundness that will in turn affect other areas of the individual life.

---

3. Towner, *Titus*, 236; Dibelius and Conzelmann, *Pastoral Epistles*, 50–51.

The intention behind these lists is to provide criteria for the kind of behavior that would be viewed as evidence for compliance to sound doctrine by older men. It communicates the following notion: "Older men, if you really are obedient to sound doctrine you will behave in these particular ways. If you are not behaving in these ways, it must be reasonably concluded that you are not obedient to sound doctrine." Paul is not suggesting that the older men are leaders, though. As was said about elder overseers, the lists constitute what is called *shared knowledge*, although it is highly likely that local leaders were selected from this category.[4] The positive qualities enunciated here were qualities that the broader society considered commendable. Paul, however, attributes such behavior to the influence of sound teaching and expects that the older men by their conduct must manifest submission to sound teaching. Here, the audience is presented with behavior that complies with sound doctrine and that would be considered good by the rest of society.

The Behavior of Older Women

In verse 3, older women (πρεσβῦτις) are required to manifest behavior compliant with sound doctrine. The adverb ὡσαύτως relates this sentence to the previous one. For older women, compliance to sound doctrine involves their behavior or demeanor (κατάστημα). The *hapax legomenon* ἱεροπρεπής refers to religious conduct or behavior. It means "to act like a sacred person."[5]

While these lists are also examples of shared knowledge, they undergo a change in the hand of the apostle. This is brought about, here and elsewhere, through the use of special religious language. The word ἱεροπρεπής is a case in point. According to Collins, it was used by classical authors to describe "priests and priestesses, religious processions and the like."[6] The author goes on to emphasize this characteristic by immediately restating it with a double negative, namely μὴ διάβολοι and μὴ οἴνῳ πολλῷ δεδουλωμέναι. Both are observable behavior, and where they are lacking, such a person cannot be said to be ἱεροπρεπής. Hence, they would not be manifesting compliance to sound doctrine. Paul employs these lists to establish objective criteria by which to measure a profession

---

4. Fee, *Titus*, 185; Towner, *Titus*, 236; Dibelius and Conzelmann, *Pastoral Epistles*, 50–51.

5. Zodhiates, *Dictionary*, s.v. "ἱεροπρεπής."

6. Collins, *Timothy and Titus*, 341.

of faith in God. Changed lives that benefit society are the only evidence to demonstrate the effect of healthy teaching.

Finally, older women must also be καλοδιδάσκαλοι. This compound word is made up of the word καλός (good) and διδάσκαλος (teacher). It is another instance of the technique of repetition. It repeats a similar idea following on from the immediate context of 2:1 and links it to earlier sections (1:9, 10). Older women must therefore be "teachers of what is good." Older women who qualify are hereby authorized to teach. They would be recognized as legitimate teachers in the church, although it would appear to be in a limited capacity.

Interestingly, the privilege to teach is made subject to the fulfillment of prior criteria and thus comes at the end of the list. This same principle applies to elder overseers who can only teach (παρακαλεῖν) if they have proven themselves in their family and private lives (1:5–9). Older women, likewise, are authorized to teach in so far as they themselves demonstrate their willingness to be taught. By way of *implicit contrast*, older women are distinguished from false teachers, since the latter are unauthorized to teach and "upset whole families" (1:11), while the former are authorized to "teach what is good." Paul employs the same argument here as in the case of older men. The behaviors that older women are expected to manifest are considered to be both Christian, as well as behavior that society associates with older women.

The Behavior of Younger Women

In verse 4, older women are made responsible to teach younger women (αἱ νέαι). The verb σωφρονίζωσιν is present active subjunctive, third-person plural. The subject is the older women. This is another interesting vocabulary switch or *use of alternative vocabulary*. Titus must speak (λάλεω), and older women on the other hand must advise, encourage, or urge (σωφρονίζω). Thus, neither Titus nor the older women must διδάσκω like the false teachers (1:11). The rhetorical objective seems to be the maintenance of a gap between legitimate and illegitimate teachers, or to avoid confusing associations between the opposing groups.

More important, though, is the focus area of the teaching, namely the family. The illegitimate teachers with their "things" (ἅ) had a subversive effect upon ὅλοι οἶκοι (1:11). In contradistinction, legitimate teaching proves to be to the advantage of families. As was mentioned elsewhere, Greco-Roman culture placed great significance on stable family institutions. According to Johnson, Christian households that ignored the mores of civil society could jeopardize the credibility of the Christian message.[7] The apostle begins by emphasizing the husband-wife and parent-child relationships (4). The family focus is perpetuated throughout this sentence, verse 5, through the use of words like οἰκουργός that contains the word οἶκος and ἐργός. This emphasis confirms the belief surrounding the importance of the family unit to the Cretans. The prior vilification section and this reference to the family suggest that people were judged based on their commitment to the progress or destruction of the family unit. The behavior commended in verse 4 would constitute a strong argument in favor of complying with sound doctrine.

Through the *repetition of key words*, the author is able to maintain a sense of coherence and momentum in the discourse. Such a word is the word σώφρων. The verbal cognate appears with reference to older women σωφρονίζωσιν. The adjective also appears in the virtue lists pertaining to older men (2:2) and elder overseers (1:8).

The reference to younger women also comprises a list of virtuous qualities that constitute *shared knowledge*. However, Paul adapts the list to achieve theological objectives through the use of religious language. For example, ἁγνός constitutes such religious language. Particular sounds and words are also intentionally repeated for emphatic effect. For example, the following words in 2:4-5, namely τὰς νέας φιλάνδρους εἶναι φιλοτέκνους σώφρονας ἁγνάς οἰκουργοὺς ἀγαθάς and ὑποτασσομένας evince the deliberate repetition of the ας sound. The same holds true for the ους sound in the following words: φιλάνδρους (εἶναι), φιλοτέκνους (σώφρονας ἁγνὰς) οἰκουργοὺς ἀγαθάς (2:4, 5). The word φίλος recurs in the two compound nouns, φιλάνδρους and φιλοτέκνους, and emphasizes endearment within the family context. Prefixing φίλος in this manner is another instance of anaphora, which was used earlier in the reference to the elder overseers (1:8). A definite link is established between the sound behavior of the younger women and the conduct of the elder overseers. When these women conduct themselves in their homes in compliance to sound doctrine, their behavior places them in company with those who teach and obey sound doctrine. No one in the audience would suggest that a wife feel any different about her husband and her children. Who would be able to discredit teaching that encourages behavior reflecting such an elevated view of the family, that encourages its adherents to

---

7. Johnson, *Paul's Delegates*, 235.

serve the family, that encourages a view of the family institution that even secular society aspires after? It would be extremely difficult to resist being persuaded to adopt behavior fitting for sound doctrine.

Verse 4 introduces another angle from which Paul argues for compliance to sound doctrine. He has argued on the basis of shared knowledge that the behavior characteristic of sound doctrine is behavior that the rest of society values. The behavior is, however, more than simple compliance to human expectations. God expects those who believe to manifest this particular kind of behavior! The ἵνα clause distinguishes the virtue lists from any secular lists. Arguing on the basis of divine authorization, Paul shows that God expects followers to behave in a specific manner so that God's word will not be maligned: ἵνα μὴ ὁ λόγος τοῦ θεοῦ βλασφημῆται. Paul's argument is that the expected behavior is of a transcendent quality, being behavior that God requires. The consequence for noncompliant behavior is also transcendent in nature, namely the maligning of the divine word. Thus, the relationship between sound doctrine and sound deeds is ultimately transcendent and presented as inseparable. Wrong behavior will impact negatively upon the ὁ λόγος τοῦ θεοῦ. In other words, more is at stake than simply the good reputation of individuals. The very reputation of the word of God (ὁ λόγος τοῦ θεοῦ) depends upon the manifestation of proper behavior by believers, especially by young wives in submission to their husbands. Just as Paul was entrusted with the manifest word of God (1:3), so now the Cretan believers are required to manifest the word of God through godly character. If they would not, God's word would be discredited (βλασφημέω) in the eyes of outsiders. The divine nature of the consequences attached to this teaching makes it necessary that believers behave in accordance to sound doctrine.

The Behavior of Young Men

Verse 6 is related to the previous category through the adverb ὡσαύτως. Thus, everything said so far also applies to young men (νεωτέροι) whom Titus must "exhort" (παρακάλει). The verb παρακάλει is another instance of a direct repetition of a word used earlier with reference to the task of elder overseers (1:9). It accentuates the proximity between Titus and the overseers and supports the idea of Titus functioning as role model to the elders. Titus must exhort the young men to be sober minded (σωφρονεῖν). This is also an instance of repetition of a similar word. Earlier, a cognate of this verb was used in connection with the role of older women who must "correct" or "teach" (σωφρονίζω) the younger women (2:4).

The Behavior of Titus

The teaching is extended in verse 7 to Titus, who must present himself (σεαυτὸν παρεχόμενος) as an example (τύπος) of good works (καλά ἔργά). The latter expression takes up a similar expression introduced in 1:16 as ἔργον ἀγαθὸν. The two words are close synonyms. The implicit contrast is undeniable: Titus, as a τύπος καλῶν ἔργων, must distinguish himself from those who are "worthless for any good work" (πρὸς πᾶν ἔργον ἀγθὸν ἀδόκιμοι) (1:16). The repetition of the adjective πᾶς is emphatic and suggests the perpetuation of the contrast between the two opposing groups. Another direct repetition occurs in the word διδασκαλία, which here is part of a prepositional phrase, in regard to which Titus must be incorruptible (ἀφθορία).

The combination of three nouns, of which two are modified, is another instance of *emphatic clustering*. The trio comprises the nouns ἀφθορία, σεμνότης, and λόγος ὑγιής, which are here modified by the adjective ἀκατάγνωστος (irreproachable). The minister of legitimate teaching must be unmistakably distinguishable from the illegitimate teachers. A more important implication is this: even Titus is not above sound teaching. His life must correspond to the doctrine. This is totally in line with everything that has been taught so far in this letter.

As in verse 5, where the integrity of the teaching (ὁ λόγος τοῦ θεοῦ) was tied to the conduct of submissive wives, so in the case of Titus the integrity of the teachers is tied to the example of Titus. The second ἵνα clause alludes to opposition (ἐξ ἐναντίας) who would be put to shame (ἐντρέπω) and prevented from saying bad things about the legitimate teachers. Most commentators understand this sentence to refer to Paul and Titus only. But it begs the question as to whether Titus, who is introduced as a "son" of the apostle, would behave in a manner that would compromise the integrity of the mission and even that of the apostle. A conclusion in the negative seems more probable, coupled with the suggestion that the pronoun ἡμεῖς represents the entire Christian movement. The use of the pronoun is a rhetorical technique to facilitate identification: to engender the us/them sentiment. The apostle speaks as an insider. In this way, he is in effect saying that if they (the opposition) badmouth any believer, they badmouth him. This part of the sentence also evinces assonance of the ε sound: ἐξ ἐναντίας ἐντραπῇ μηδὲν ἔχων λέγειν περὶ ἡμῶν. This is for emphatic purposes, to highlight the serious consequences of compromising conduct. Believers must conduct themselves in compliance with sound doctrine because the apostle expects this behavior from them. This constitutes an argument based upon apostolic authorization.

The Behavior of Slaves

In verses 9-10, the behavior of Christian slaves (δοῦλοι) is addressed. There are several instances of direct repetition from earlier sections that ties this section to the content of the entire discourse. It includes the following words: δοῦλος (1:1), ὑποτάσσω (2:4), ἀντιλέγω (1:9), πᾶς (1:15, 16; 2:7), πίστος (1:1, 4, 6, 9, 13; 2:2), ἀγαθός (1:16; 2:5), διδασκαλία (1:9, 11; 2:1, 7), σωτήρ (1:3, 4), θεός (1:1 [twice], 7, 16; 2:5), and the expression σωτήρ ἡμῶν θεός (1:3). The rhetorical significance of this extensive repetition lies in the parallels and comparisons that are drawn through it. It is also important for the cohesion of this unit.

Paul introduced himself as a δοῦλος in 1:1. This self-signification softens any negative connotation associated with this word. In fact, it places the master-slave relationship in a positive light, thus serving an ameliorative purpose. Furthermore, Paul's identification with those at the bottom end of the social ladder would do much to commend him and especially the content of this letter to the congregation. On another level, Paul takes the place of a role model as he demonstrates his obedience to God. There is, therefore, a sense in which Paul is speaking here not as a high-handed apostle but rather as a fellow slave in submission to the great Master. It is from this perspective that he can "urge" slaves in the congregation to follow his example. The rest of the congregation would be hard pressed to reject those who are lower in the social order, since they would then have to reject even Paul. Thus, through the use of this word, the apostle is facilitating harmony within the congregation.

Slaves must "submit" (ὑποτάσσω) to their masters in the same way that younger women are expected to "submit" (ὑποτάσσω) to their husbands (2:4). By contrast, the false teachers have been vilified as ἀνυπότακτοι (1:10). Through paronomasia, Paul establishes, on the one hand, a positive connection between the various groups of believers while on the other hand facilitating a contrast with the opposition. The paronomasia maintains the polarity between those who are "sound" and those who are "unsound." Paul makes a very persuasive case for the adoption of sound doctrine and the resultant compliant behavior since sound doctrine manifests as ὑποτάσσω, while false doctrine manifests as behavior vilified as ἀνυπότακτος. The audience must choose. Another word that was used to describe the opposition is repeated in this address to slaves, namely ἀντιλέγω. The repetition serves a similar objective as the earlier word, namely to discourage such behavior by drawing the parallel with the false teachers. This is an instance of negative role modeling or stigmatization. By associating this word with the opposition, it becomes negative; an attitude or behavior that must be avoided. Paul does the same, in a positive sense, through the word δοῦλος.

While the false teachers are "worthless for any good work" (πᾶν ἔργον ἀγαθὸν ἀδόκιμοι), the slaves must "show/demonstrate all good faith" (πᾶσαν πίστιν ἐνδεικνυμένοι ἀγαθήν). The disparity between the two groups is intensified by the work/faith antithesis. Slaves who obey the legitimate teaching demonstrate by that their alignment to "*the* faith." The rhetorical objective is to alienate the false teachers through stigmatization and to attract the believers through positive association with those who demonstrate compliance to sound doctrine by good behavior.

The third ἵνα clause, 2:9, is positive, unlike the previous two that are phrased in such a way as to discourage the negative consequences of noncompliance to sound doctrine (2:5, 6). God expects behavior compliant to sound doctrine because it "adorns" or "beautifies" (κοσμέω) the teaching of God (ἡ διδασκαλία ἡ τοῦ σωτῆρος ἡμῶν θεοῦ). This is the third example of an argument based upon divine authorization. The triple repetition of this argument is in itself an emphatic strategy. It emphasizes the truth that these behavioral characteristics are mandatory, not primarily because the rest of society expects it, but rather because God expects people to behave in these ways.

The apostle reserves the highest commendation for the lowest sector of society by ascribing to them the honor of adorning the doctrine of God. The divine nature of the teaching is emphasized by referring to it as belonging to or originating from God (τοῦ ... θεοῦ). This reference to God takes up a theme introduced in the salutation. In the present instance, it serves as a transitionary device that will be developed in the subsequent section. In this way, the apostle systematically ties the various sections together into a unified whole.

The exhortation, to adorn the doctrine of God, is a beautiful variation of rhetorical strategy. When one wants to persuade, it is good to present a positive challenge to people that encourages the desired outcome instead of merely speaking in prohibitory tones.

There is clearly a parallel between the reference in 2:5 to ὁ λόγος τοῦ θεοῦ and ἡ διδασκαλία ... τοῦ ... θεοῦ. On the one hand, the expressions are synonymous. On the other hand, they reveal a contrast and progression within the section. In the respective sentences, the verbs that are employed progress from negative (βλασφημέω) to positive (κοσμέω). Additionally, there is development in the theological dimension of the two sentences. The reference τοῦ θεοῦ in 2:5 becomes σωτῆρος ἡμῶν θεοῦ. Finally, the presence of the personal pronoun is an instance of inclusive language or the us/them reference. Again, Paul cannot be understood to imply that God is only the Savior of himself and Titus. Everything that has been said about the apostle's use of vocabulary militates against such a narrow interpretation. There appears, therefore, to be an evident theological progression that will climax in the next section. It is as if Paul has not said everything he wants to say; he wants to ground the teaching expressed in chapter 2. This is exactly what he is going to do in the ensuing section.

CONCLUSION

In this section, the dominant rhetorical strategy is *to persuade the Cretans that personal conduct compliant with sound doctrine is compulsory and should characterize all believers.* The comprehensive nature of sound doctrine is demonstrated by applying it to various sectors of the social strata of Crete. Even Titus is not excluded from the influence of legitimate teaching.

Two lines of argument are used to achieve the dominant objective. The first argument is based upon the notion of shared knowledge. Christians must manifest the right behavior because the rest of society also considers such behavior to be good. The next line of argument is transcendent in nature. The behavior that believers must manifest is behavior that God expects from people (5, 6, 9). The repetition of this line of reasoning suggests that the apostle considers it to be more authoritative and binding upon believers. In other words, the behavior that believers must manifest exceeds the maintenance of a good public image—they must live up to the expectations of God!

Through rhetorical techniques like repetition, behavior compliant with sound doctrine is demonstrated to characterize all believers; thus, the correspondence between the behavioral characteristics of older men and elder overseers and between Paul being a slave of God and the Christian slaves in Crete. The positive effect of Christian behavior in the home is negatively contrasted with the damaging effect of false teachers (1:11). Similarly, the behavior of "teaching what is good" (2:3) spoken about older women is contrasted with the false teachers who "teach things not necessary" (1:11). These techniques maintain the tension between "sound" and "unsound," forcing the audience to choose a position.

Other rhetorical techniques used in this section include inclusive language, paronomasia, role modeling, and stigmatization, while the use of implicit contrast occurs constantly.

The superiority of legitimate teaching over against illegitimate teaching is a secondary outcome of this section. Thus, sound doctrine must be embraced and the corresponding behavior must be manifested because it is superior to false doctrine. This superiority is more implicit rather than explicit in the text. Sound teaching benefits the family institution, by respecting the authority of the husband. This is the same argument used with reference to slaves. Furthermore, some *theological progression* is discernible from the references to God and this paves the way for the next section. The expression σωτῆρ ἡμῶν θεοῦ is taken up here, having first appeared in the salutation, and it serves as a transitional device that will be developed in the next section.

7

Titus 2:11–15

Emphasizing the Divine Basis of Obedience to Sound Doctrine

THE DOMINANT RHETORICAL OBJECTIVE in this section is to emphasize the divine basis of obedience to sound doctrine. In the previous section, Paul highlighted the relationship between sound doctrine and deeds compliant with the doctrine. Deeds corresponding to sound doctrine were shown to comply with the expectations of the rest of society. In verses 5 and 10, he alluded to the transcendent nature of the prescribed behavior, namely that it is good behavior that God expects from people. He furthermore emphasized the benefits that legitimate teaching has for the broad spectrum of the congregation as well as the beneficial influence of legitimate teaching upon social institutions like the family and servant-master relationships. Now, Paul is going to proverbially "clinch the deal" by a final argument. He is going to justify the divine expectation for sound behavior in accordance with sound doctrine by arguing on the basis of the divine origin of this teaching. Not only is the behavior in line with that which God expects, but so is the doctrine that prescribes the behavior. Paul is now arguing that God is the one teaching the doctrine, making the doctrine and the behavior inseparable. The teaching as well as the Teacher are transcendent and must therefore be obeyed because they are not of human origin. This line of reasoning stresses the obligatory nature of sound doctrine upon the minds of the Cretans. In other words, sound doctrine must be obeyed because it is the exact opposite of "the commandments of men" (1:14). Not to obey the doctrine and therefore not to manifest these particular behavioral characteristics is tantamount to disobedience to God. This is the point that Paul seems to develop in this section.

Verses 11–14 are one sentence in the original Greek. This is the second unusually long sentence in this letter. The use of such a long sentence is in itself a strategic rhetorical technique used to emphasize the material communicated by it. Fee calls it a "marvelous passage" with "so much theological grist that it is easy to analyze it solely on its own merits and thereby overlook its place in the context of the letter."[1] Most commentators appear not to see any relationship between the theological references in verses 5 and 9 and those in the present section but correctly recognize the theological import of the section and its explanatory function with regard to 2:2–10.[2] The section is related to the previous section by the use of the conjunction γάρ, which here functions in an explanatory capacity. A number of linguistic parallels tie these two sections together. For example, the words in verse 10, τοῦ . . . θεοῦ and the proximate word, σωτήρ, are repeated in verse 11. There is also a transition from τὴν διδασκαλίαν . . . τοῦ . . . θεοῦ (2:10) to ἡ χάρις τοῦ θεοῦ (2:11).

The author employs repetition, unique vocabulary, and other rhetorical techniques to accomplish his objectives in this section. The dominant rhetorical objective is to emphasize the theological foundation of the conduct expounded in 2:2–10, by highlighting the divine origin of the teaching. The teaching should be embraced because it is not a human idea.

The best explanation for what Paul is doing in this instance is the analogy of an eavesdropper. Paul is ostensibly in a conversation with Titus. Hultgren describes this as "talking past" Titus to the community.[3] Paul's conversation with Titus is conducted in such a manner as to invite or attract others to become part of it. While there is no direct communication with the Cretan believers at any stage in this discourse, they are an integral part of it. This explains the use of inclusive language, which is perpetuated throughout this section.

---

1. Fee, *Titus*, 193.

2. Mounce, *Pastoral Epistles*, 433; Quinn, *Letter to Titus*, 162; Johnson, *Paul's Delegates*, 240–41.

3. Hultgren, *Timothy, Titus*, 19, 20.

The Universal Appearance of Grace in the Past

In verse 11, the transcendent nature of the teaching that mandates the behavior is emphasized first. The transformation that the Cretans are required to manifest (vv. 2–10) is explicable with reference to the appearance of the saving grace of God (Ἐπεφάνη γὰρ ἡ χάρις τοῦ θεοῦ σωτήριος). It appeared to all men or people (πᾶσιν ἀνθρώποις), including the Cretans at some point in the past, as suggested by the aorist tense of the verb ἐπιφαίνω. The universal appearance and inclusiveness of divine grace is a key emphasis in this part of the sentence. Furthermore, the combination of the verb ἐπιφαίνω and the adjective πᾶς suggests that this event was neither a clandestine occasion nor limited to a particular group. According to Quinn,[4] the expression πᾶς ἄνθρωπος is used by Paul outside of the Pastorals for polemical purposes. Thus, the use of the adjective πᾶς here suggests a polemical purpose against illegitimate teaching, which may have encouraged mythological, secretive, and exclusive tendencies. The immediate context confirms such an interpretation since Paul takes great pains to specify the different categories that can be found in the church. The lowest category, namely "slaves," is presented positively, being afforded the privilege to "adorn the doctrine of God" (2:10).

The Particular Instruction of Grace in the Present

In verse 12, the expression παιδεύουσα ἡμᾶς introduces a limitation. The participle form of the verb παιδεύω is present active. Thus, grace continues to instruct in the present. Grace now, at present, instructs (παιδεύω) only a very particular group, namely "us." Again, this cannot merely refer to Paul and Titus. Instead, it is another instance of *inclusive language* that includes the "eavesdroppers." By using inclusive language, Paul is clearly showing his approval and submission to this teaching or instruction. He is also in complete community with those who are so instructed. Commentators debate the interpretation of παιδεύω, arguing that it denotes both chastisement or discipline and education.[5] A punitive connotation does not suit the immediate context. Instead, the focus of the chapter is upon instruction or sound doctrine, in which case

---

4. Quinn, *Letter to Titus*, 163.

5. Mounce, *Pastoral Epistles*, 423, 424; Johnson, *Paul's Delegates*, 241; Quinn, *Letter to Titus*, 163, 164.

"discipline" or "education" is the better interpretation. Thus, grace is now "educating us."[6] It is also explicable as an instance of the use of a synonymous expression to differentiate legitimate from illegitimate teaching. Additionally, this verb suggests the notion of family, since instruction would first occur in the family. If this interpretation is tenable, then Paul's use of the third-person pronoun is a good strategy to facilitate identification and community.

A new aspect to Paul's strategy is the use of personification. He applies this rhetorical technique to the concept of grace, which appeared (v. 11) and now instructs (v. 12) the believers. Kelly does not interpret grace as personified but prefers instead to interpret it as "God's free favor, the spontaneous goodness by which he intervenes to help deliver men."[7] The present tense of the verb makes the teaching act real, personal, and imminent or "contemporary and continuous."[8] Obedience to the instruction becomes obedience to "someone," rather than something. This is a very persuasive angle. Grace offers the complete opposite of what the false teachers have to offer. By formulating the proposition in this way, the appeal of sound doctrine is highlighted, making the argument for compliance to it even more persuasive. Furthermore, the personification of grace reinforces the notion of accountability. Paul's audience would have been familiar with the concept of discipline and instruction. By phrasing it in this manner, the point that religious obedience demands the same obedience is driven home.

The significance of what grace accomplishes is emphasized through assonance of the vowel α, which recurrs in verse 12: παιδεύουσα ἡμᾶς ἵνα ἀρνησάμενοι τὴν ἀσέβειαν καὶ τὰς κοσμικὰς ἐπιθυμίας.

Furthermore, through the direct repetition of the verb ἀρνέομαι the author creates an implicit contrast. Those instructed by grace deny "irreverence" or "ungodliness" and "worldly desires" (τὴν ἀσέβειαν καὶ τὰς κοσμικὰς ἐπιθυμίας) whereas the false teachers are vilified as denying God (1:16). In this way, the diametrical opposition between the two groups is highlighted. The repetition serves to maintain the polarity, keeping the two groups at opposite ends and closing the door for any compromise or endorsement. The word ἀσέβεια constitutes use of religious language and is the opposite of εὐσέβεια. The implication is that sound doctrine

6. Classen, *Rhetorical Criticism*, 58.

7. Kelly, *Commentary*, 244.

8. Johnson, *Paul's Delegates*, 240.

does not have its origin in man, and the choice of vocabulary encourages the denial of ἀσέβεια or, positively, the manifestation of εὐσέβεια in the present life. This argument links up with the salutation where faith and knowledge of "God's elect" is said to be for the purpose of εὐσέβεια (1:1). To thus claim to know God (and be instructed by God's grace) requires a denial of everything that would contradict that claim. Thus, the two are mutually exclusive since students of divine grace cannot synchronically manifest both ἀσέβεια and εὐσέβεια.

Paronomasia is also evident from the two cognate words κοσμικάς (v. 12) and κοσμῶσιν (v. 10). The latter verb is a positive action that slaves must perform in regard to the teaching of God and is therefore encouraged. The former relates to the world in a negative sense and must therefore be denied. The paronomasia serves to maintain the polarity between "sound" and "not sound," which leaves the audience with a choice to make.

Another key concern revolves around the difference between legitimate and illegitimate teaching. There is an almost concentric or circular progression detectable with regard to the theme of teaching. Through the use of concentric or circular progression, the dichotomy between legitimacy and illegitimacy is maintained. The progression becomes evident as different categories of legitimate teaching sources are identified. In chapter 1, it includes Paul, Titus and the elder overseers. In chapter 2, it again includes Titus and extends to the ministry of older women. Finally, the readers are informed about the manifestation of divine grace that appeared and now teaches. There is a sense in which the argument has gone full circle, if we take into consideration the opening verses of the letter where the manifestation of the divine word is mentioned. In the present section, the teaching grace of God is presented as another manifestation of the divine word.

The juxtaposition of κοσμικάς ἐπιθυμίας and σωφρόνως (v. 12) highlights the contrast between that which must be denied and that which must be practiced. The latter word is another instance of repetition. This word has been used positively throughout the section and in earlier parts of the letter. It now forms part of another *emphatic cluster* along with δικαίως καὶ εὐσεβῶς. Quinn[9] correctly identifies assonance and the rhyming –ῶς of the adverbs, the polysyndeton, and the adverbial usage. He proposes that this cluster is clearly emphatic and suggestive of the

9. Quinn, *Letter to Titus*, 168.

inseparability of these qualities in Christian living. Thus, in the instruction of grace, the three qualities come together to form a unity characteristic of those who profess to know God. Each of the three words in this cluster has been used previously, but this is the first time they are combined. In this regard, one can almost refer to them as *doubly emphatic*.

In the case of δικαίως, it should be noted that the adjective δίκαιος was used first with reference to elder overseers (1:8). It now is a characteristic of all who are instructed by grace. Its repetition serves to enhance the identification and community of the students of grace. Thus, if the believers manifest conduct corresponding to sound doctrine, they are in community with those identified in 1:5–9 and not with the opposition who are incapable of manifesting δίκαιος.

In the case of εὐσεβῶς, it should be noted that the emphatic repetition and recollection of εὐσέβεια, first raised in 1:1, makes an important point regarding the consistency of the divine intent. The purpose of the apostolic ministry was for the sake of godliness (1:1). The appearance of grace, who instructs "her" students in godliness, emphasizes that Paul is not introducing anything new. He expects the Cretans to be in total agreement with the divine mandate. Absolute consensus exists between what the apostle is appointed to do and what grace is instructing the believers to do. The fact that the audience can observe this consistency adds to the persuasiveness of Paul's argument.

Paul thus gives "shared knowledge" a theological nuance to the extent that he attributes the manifestation of these virtues in those instructed by grace to a transcendent or a divine act. There is therefore nothing "ordinary" about these characteristics. Put differently, "civilisation, and culture are not necessarily 'natural' and . . . the habits of the heart that build communities of meaning and of meaningful relationships can be forgotten and lost or abused and destroyed. Sometimes, civilisation needs to be taught for the first time to the savage heart or relearned by the heart grown savage."[10] Through "religious language," the theological nature of the appropriate conduct is intensified, while, by implicit contrast, the positive qualities are shown to be in direct contrast to the three in the vilification section (1:12). What these and other rhetorical techniques do is to press home the distinction between "sound" and "not sound" and to impress upon the audience the inseparable relationship between doctrine and deeds: the false teachers are unsound because

---

10. Johnson, *Paul's Delegates*, 240.

of their deeds, and their deeds are unsound because of their doctrine! Likewise, divine and apostolic authorized teachers are sound because of their deeds, and their deeds are sound because of their doctrine.

Another instance of the rhetorical technique of inclusive language is evident in the verb ζήσωμεν, "we might live." It includes all of those who are instructed by grace, whose lives give evidence of being lived "sensibly, righteously and godly." The technique enhances the sense of community and presents Paul as one who is teachable and in submission to the instruction of divine grace. Furthermore, it adds to his credibility and facilitates his rapport with the audience.

The temporal phrase, ἐν τῷ νῦν αἰῶνι, "in the now (present) age," recalls and relates to the reference in the salutation (1:2) about God's divine promise, which was before the ages. This enhances the sense of coherence between the letter's various sections. More importantly, it is very emphatic about the implications legitimate teaching has for this present life. The sentence demonstrates multiple time dimensions moving from past to present and, in verse 13, to future. This heightens the temporal momentum that is evident in this section. The motivation behind this notion is clearly to illustrate to the Cretans that their conduct does not take place in a vacuum. Their positive conduct in the present is attributable to the historical intervention of God.

Verse 13 takes up the future dimension that is also present in the salutation. The ἐλπίς ζωῆς αἰωνίου in 1:2 now becomes ἡ μακαρία ἐλπίς, "blessed hope" which Paul ties to the fact of the return of Jesus Christ, identified here as God. The past, present, and future time references place the congregation between two appearances: the first was when divine grace appeared in the past; the second appearance will be in the future when Jesus Christ will return. Complying to sound doctrine with corresponding behavior is not only the wisest option because of its divine origin. Right (or wrong) behavior has implications for the future: those who manifest compliant behavior do so because they demonstrate thereby that they have a "blessed hope." Negatively, the implication is that those who do not manifest obedience to the instruction of grace must remember that Jesus Christ is going to appear again in the future. In other words, the "now" or "present age" is the age of compliance to sound doctrine.

The divinity of Jesus Christ relates directly to the salutation. Elsewhere, I have indicated my concurrence with the interpretation that the expression "our great God and Savior" applies to Jesus Christ (see [x-ref]). The reference to Jesus as ἡμῶν is another example of "inclusive language." If Paul's arguments in 2:2–10 can be described as sociological or even missiological,[11] his argument in this section can be described as theological. Paul amasses theological terms in this part of the sentence, in order to convince his audience of the transcendent implications of legitimate teaching. The transcendent nature of sound doctrine places it in a class of its own and makes it superior to "Jewish myths and the commandments of men" (1:14). The evidence serves as proof for the insistence upon adherence and submission to sound doctrine. Through the use of inclusive language, Paul demonstrates that he himself submits to the teaching and lives as one anticipating the return of Jesus Christ.

Several commentators agree that this section functions as explanatory to the preceding instructions.[12] Rhetorically, however, more is involved. Paul is not only saying: "The reason I want you to do this (vv. 2–10) is because of this (vv. 11–14)." Instead, he is claiming: "The teaching that I want you to embrace and the behavior I want you to manifest are superior to what those presumptive fellows are trying to sell you. Their teaching originates from a human mind. Just look at the way they live! This doctrine that we advocate is divine. If you do not accept it, you are in direct opposition to God. It is a choice between teaching that is human and teaching that is divine." It leaves the hearer or reader in the awkward position of having to decide. It offers no neutral grounds.

The vocabulary selected in this section places the emphasis on the uniqueness and the distinctiveness of God's people. There is a sense in which Paul almost indirectly uses the language to point to the ideal. He does not tell or specify to the Cretans that they are a special people, that *they* have been chosen of God. Instead, the emphasis appears to be on the notion of privilege to have been chosen *by God*.

There are in verse 14 two final instances of inclusive language. Jesus is said to have given himself "for us," to redeem "us" (ὃς ἔδωκεν ἑαυτὸν ὑπὲρ ἡμῶν ἵνα λυτρώσηται ἡμᾶς). The emphasis in the final verse is on the activity of the divine. Having identified Jesus Christ as God "our Savior," the sentence goes on to describe what he has done: he gave himself for us, in order that he might save us. This *us* then becomes a

---

11. Collins, *Timothy and Titus*, 12–13; Karris, *Pastoral Epistles*, 113, 116.

12. Demarest, *Timothy, Titus*, 320; Johnson, *Paul's Delegates*, 240; Clark, Discourse Structure, 111.

"unique and peculiar people, zealous for good works" (2:14). The reality of the divine intervention thus constitutes the reason why Christians or Cretan believers ought to be characterized by the performance of good works compliant with sound doctrine.

The final reason why the Cretans are expected to manifest the stipulated behavior has to do with their transformation. They have been changed by the divine intervention, namely the appearance of grace. They have become in Jesus Christ the objects of divine interest, when he gave himself for them (ὃς ἔδωκεν ἑαυτὸν ὑπὲρ ἡμῶν). The inclusive language in this part is also emphatic. They are no longer mere Cretans, but the people of God—God's own peculiar people (ἑαυτῷ λαός περιούσιος). Their identity and consequently their natures have been changed. They have been made God's own "unique people." This expression reinforces the communal sense prevalent in this section. Thus, when Cretan believers perform good deeds, in other words, when they obey the instructions of divine grace, they are acting consistently with their new character. Together with the inclusive language, this becomes a compelling reason to conform, since it is implied that failure to do so has consequences; for example, it could result in exclusion and loss of privileges. God redeemed (λυτρόομαι) and cleansed (καθαρίζω) them from all lawlessness (ἀπὸ πάσης ἀνομίας). This is an instance of a divine authorization argument based on the notion of *the right of the divine* or *the divine prerogative*. God has a right over the Cretans. God purchased them and God cleansed them. By implication, therefore, they do not belong to themselves, but to God.

The irony lies in the notion that the Jewish segment of the false teachers would probably have wanted to get the Cretans to submit to the law of ritual purity. Here, Paul stresses that it is God who cleanses from lawlessness. Hence, they can no longer act in a way that contradicts all that they have become through Jesus Christ. In fact, they should be "zealous for good works" (ζηλωτὴς καλῶν ἔργων). The argument is based on the notion of *irreconcilable conduct*. This is the opposite of the false teachers (and their disciples) who are "worthless for any good work" (πᾶν ἔργον ἀγαθὸν ἀδόκιμοι). The choice is clear: whether you are of God or not of God will be shown by your works. The contrast could not be more blatant than this.

The section closes with the apostle reiterating his affirmation of Titus's ministry.[13] In 2:15, the apostle reaffirms the ministry of Titus. The sentence is a more developed and emphatic rejoinder to verse 1. Opening with ταῦτα (these things), it reveals another *emphatic cluster*: λάλει καὶ παρακάλει καὶ ἔλεγχε.

The demonstrative pronoun ταῦτα functions vis-à-vis the relative pronoun in 1:11. The false teachers teach "things" and do so without authorization. Titus, however, is authorized to teach and is told what to teach. This affirmation not only involves affirming Titus; instead it involves the apostolic affirmation of sound doctrine. The congregation has just been instructed not only to manifest but also to identify and evaluate sound doctrine; they have been reminded what sound doctrine "looks" like. The reference is clearly to the content of chapter 2. Paul seems to be saying: "Anyone who does not teach 'these things' that Titus will be teaching is not a teacher of sound doctrine. Beware!"

All the verbs in the emphatic cluster are in the present tense and in the imperative mood. They can also be considered *doubly emphatic* because each one is repeated throughout the letter. Their occurrence here is exceptional since they all appear together in one sentence. The first verb, λάλει, links the concluding and opening sentences of this chapter thereby forming a tidy border around the teaching section. The next verb, παρακάλει, is a repetition from 1:9 and 2:6. The latter reference is also applicable to Titus. The former occurs as part of the duties of elders and correlates the ministry of Titus to that of elder overseers. The only way elders are going to know how to perform this ministry is by observing Titus. The final of the trio, ἔλεγχε, occurs in 1:9 and in 1:13. As with the previous word, ἔλεγχε also links the ministry of Titus to that of the elder overseers (1:9). Both occurrences of the word appear in the context of rebuking the opposition, first by the elder overseers (1:9) then by Titus (1:13). Thus, by means of this verbal association, ministerial parallels are drawn between Titus's ministry and that of the future leaders of the church at Crete.

The prepositional phrase, μετὰ πάσης ἐπιταγῆς, is a further validation of Titus's mandate at Crete. The word ἐπιταγή recalls what was said earlier (1:3) with reference to God. It seems to suggest that just as Paul

---

13. Wendland, "Let No One," 348, considers verse 15 the organizational "keystone" or "nucleus" for the structure of the letter. This interpretation does not, however, consider the linear or chronological flow of the text.

was commanded by God, that is, by divine authorization, so now by apostolic authorization, Titus must exercise all command or authority.

The final command, μηδείς σου περιφρονείτω, is an instance of tautology. Paul is restating the same thing in different words, that is, negatively, for the purpose of emphasis. Wendland[14] argues that the expression is intended to reinforce the authority with which Titus is expected to execute his ministry in Crete. It is clear that the rhetorical objective in verse 15 is the apostolic reaffirmation of Titus's ministry in the Cretan context.

CONCLUSION

In this section, Paul's dominant rhetorical objective is *to emphasize the divine basis of obedience to sound doctrine*. His argument is based upon the divine origin of right teaching. The appearance of the grace of God was the watershed moment in the lives of the Cretans. The historical intervention of the divine is emphasized through the use of time references. The past, present, and future perspectives contribute to the sense of temporal momentum that permeates the letter. It also provides a context for the conduct that is enjoined upon the believers. They must demonstrate in the present the required behavior because something happened in the past. They continue in this behavior because of something else that will happen in the future, namely the return of the Lord Jesus Christ. The basic arguments rallied involve irreconcilable conduct and the divine prerogative or the right of the divine. In terms of the former argument, the Cretans are compelled to act in accordance to their new natures. In the case of the latter argument, God has a right over the Cretans and can therefore dictate divinely required conduct to them.

The origin of this teaching lies in the divine, since grace itself is teaching the believers. The usual rhetorical techniques in this section include inclusive language, implicit contrasting, emphatic clustering, and religious language. Another technique is personification, by means of which grace is presented as the one who is teaching all believers. The word *teach* (παιδεύω) is a totally new and distinctive word that suggests the notion of family.

Having dealt with issue of origin, Paul proceeds in the same sentence to insist upon compliance to the teaching based on the argument

---

14. Wendland, "Let No One," 33.

of the *divine prerogative*. Christ gave himself for them, purchased them, and cleansed them. By implication, therefore, they do not belong to themselves anymore. God has a right to require specific behavior from those whom God has made God's own.

Paul proceeds by arguing for compliant behavior based on the notion of irreconcilable *conduct*. Through divine intervention, the Cretan believers have been changed, and therefore their behavior must testify to this transformation. They are now God's people, recipients of God's favor. Consequently, a propensity toward good works should be the natural manifestation of this reality. Through the combination of the communal reference to God's "unique people," and inclusive language, the author exploits the desire to belong. Negatively, it amounts to use of the fear of exclusion to enforce compliant behavior. The persuasive effect of this strategy is that the hearers would be more inclined to demonstrate compliant behavior. They are not given any options. The argument is presented in such a compelling manner that no compromises are possible; no neutral ground is offered. Sound doctrine is of transcendent origin, while the false teaching comes from men. Behavior contrary to what grace teaches is behavior that God does not approve of. Believers presently live between the two appearances, both of which have implications for their lives. The section concludes with a final apostolic affirmation of Titus's ministry as well as that of the elders. What brings this about is the doubly emphatic cluster that draws close parallels between the ministries of Titus and that of elder overseers.

8

Titus 3:1–2

Persuading the Cretans of the Compulsory Treatment of All Unbelievers in a Manner Consistent with Sound Doctrine

SEVERAL COMMENTATORS CONSIDER THIS section as a continuation of the instructions given in 2:1–10.[1] Mounce even views it as a repetition of 2:1–14.[2] It is, however, also possible to view this as a new section that introduces a different rhetorical objective. Paul's dominant rhetorical objective can be summarized as *persuading the Cretans that they must treat all unbelievers in a manner consistent with sound doctrine.* Commentators agree that the pronoun αὐτούς refers to all believers. However, Quinn interprets the pronoun as a reference to what he calls the Jewish Christian opponents of 1:10, 16.[3] Some differences are, however, noticeable between these two sections. The earlier section in 2:1–10 distinguished between various categories of believers, with instructions specific to each group. In the present section, the pronoun αὐτούς suggests that the earlier categories are now viewed as the collective group of Cretan believers.

Thus far, Titus has been given many instructions. The verb ὑπομίμνῃσκω, in this instance, indicates another aspect of his ministry as a teacher of sound doctrine. It is also in the imperative second-person singular like that of 2:15 and expresses a continuation of the ministry of

---

1. Johnson, *Paul's Delegates*, 246; Quinn, *Letter to Titus*, 182; Fee, *Titus*, 200; Collins, *Timothy and Titus*, 356.

2. Mounce, *Pastoral Epistles*, 443.

3. Quinn, *Letter to Titus*, 182.

Titus, who here represents legitimate teaching. The choice of this word to describe an aspect of legitimate teaching could indicate a caution against accepting novel teachings. Paul turns the attention in this section to the whole congregation. The pronoun αὐτούς refers to everyone who was mentioned in 2:1–10. The use of the pronoun signifies a comprehensive expansion of the teaching ministry. Whereas in the previous section the apostle specified particular categories of people, he now includes everyone by using the pronoun.

Verses 1–2 are a single sentence in Greek. It contains a list of seven virtues. This is counterbalanced in verse 3 by a list of seven vices. The strategy that the apostle adopts to persuade his audience consists of an argument based on *an appeal to the prior knowledge of his audience* to motivate them to manifest the ensuing list of positive behavioral traits. The verb ὑπομίμνησκω represents a possible variation in vocabulary to distinguish the ministry of Titus from that of the false teachers. The function of this verb is open to several interpretive possibilities. It, first of all, seems to introduce another dimension of legitimate teaching, namely "remembering." Next, the use of the verb suggests a polemic against novel teachings. It also suggests the succession of legitimate ministry. In other words, if sound doctrine is consistent and void of novelties, it becomes transmittable from one generation to the next by a succession of teachers. The task of new teachers would therefore involve reminding the congregations. This implies that the audience is expected to be familiar with the teaching, since one reminds people of things that they already know. In other words, they have had prior exposure to the instructions that are about to follow, having already received instruction in it. It is as if the apostle is saying, "Here are things that people already know but need to be reminded of again." In 1:13, Titus had to "rebuke" or "reprove" them (ἐλεγχειν αὐτούς), with particular reference to the false teachers. In the present sentence, the verb ὑπομίμνησκω has as its direct object the pronoun αὐτούς. Titus is hereby authorized to take up the task of reminding the believers. He is given the responsibility to continue what someone else has begun. This is therefore another instance of apostolic affirmation of Titus's ministry, through the use of an alternative verb in the imperative mode.

The choice of the verb demands further explanation. "Remind them" implies knowledge preexistent to the hearers. In other words, at some stage, when they were first exposed to the gospel, the Cretans were exposed to this information. It thus constitutes an argument based on the existence of prior knowledge or an argument based on the appeal to memory. This argument emphasizes the temporal priority of legitimate teaching that the Cretans were initially exposed to, over against illegitimate teaching, which must have come afterward. This argument thus puts the hearers in a position to evaluate the veracity of legitimate teaching. They are able to measure what they are being taught now with what they have been taught previously. The motive could be to prove the consistency of legitimate teaching over against the implied inconsistency of illegitimate teaching. Thus, by implication, the Cretans have been practicing legitimate teaching all along and are now in danger of forsaking that which they have embraced. If the Cretans do not embrace and practice sound doctrine, they are implicitly acting against themselves. Their behavior would be interpreted as self-contradictory.

Another interpretation would be to view it as a polemic against illegitimate teaching. The latter could have encouraged the people, namely the Cretans, to conduct themselves in a manner contrary to the good conduct that is being advocated in this section. Whatever the content of the illegitimate teaching might have been, its implications may have involved encouraging the believers to conduct themselves in a manner unbecoming of good citizens.

The appeal to prior knowledge relates to knowledge of what is considered positively by the secular society. They must therefore be reminded of that behavior which they have known to be commendable and which society admires. They are to make a positive contribution toward society, namely demonstrable submissive conduct. In other words, they must not abandon that conduct which they have known to be good. The discourse suggests the existence of a need to remind the believers lest they make themselves guilty of conduct that would elicit a negative response from the rest of society and government authorities—conduct that would make them appear separatist, exclusivist, and insurrectionary since it is to the ἀρχαί ἐξουσίαι that they must submit. This interpretation seems to make the best sense in the present context and explains the structure of the section: seven virtues (v. 1–2) followed by seven vices (v. 3) with several supportive rhetorical techniques, including asyndeton, direct repetition, assonance, and paronomasia.

Believers must submit to the ἀρχαί ἐξουσίαι. Commentators struggle with the asyndeton here. This leaves them to interpret the two nouns very differently. Most commentators treat ἀρχαί as a modifier, translating it as "governing/government authorities" or "legitimate rulers."[4] Some commentators supply a conjunction and treat the two adjectives as separate, for example, "rulers and authorities."[5] Bernard translates this literally as "to rulers, to authorities."[6] There would be no need to add a conjunction since the absence of the conjunction conforms to the structure of this entire section. Furthermore, asyndeton is a rhetorical technique that features regularly in this letter.

The absence of conjunctions in both lists is rather conspicuous. The asyndeton is for emphatic purposes. It accentuates the interrelatedness or inseparableness of the various elements that make up these lists. The cohesiveness is enhanced by the use of the infinitive mode in the first five verbs of verses 1 and 2: ὑποάσσεσθαι, πειθαρχεῖν, εἶναι, βλασφημεῖν, and εἶναι. The list is completed with two adjectives, ἐπιεικεῖς and πραΰτητα.

The relationship between believers and the governing authorities is one that ought to be characterized by submission on the part of believers. The verb ὑποάσσεσθαι is an instance of paronomasia and a repetition from 2:5 and 2:9. Just as in the context of the home, the wife's relationship to her husband is characterized by submission and in the context of employment the servant's relationship is characterized by submission to the master, so in the context of society the believer's relationship to government authorities must be characterized by submission. The progression in the theme of submission is remarkable when considered in the light of 2:1–3:1. It involves the distinct realms where submission is required, namely in the home, then in the workplace, culminating with submission in the public sector. Then there is progression in the three levels of recognized authority: first to a husband, then to a master, and finally to governing authorities. There is also progression in regard to the sectors from which submission can be expected: Christian wives, Christian slaves, and Christian citizens. Thus, irrespective of whether you are a wife or a slave, a Christian must demonstrate submission to all authority. Paradoxically, the false teachers are called ἀνυπότακτοι (1:10) while the children of elder overseers must not manifest this characteristic (1:6). A compound noun, it has as its root the word ὑποτάσσω. The paronomasia serves to facilitate an implicit contrast between those who

---

4. Quinn, *Letter to Titus*, 178; Fee, *Titus*, 201; Collins, *Timothy and Titus*, 357.

5. Johnson, *Paul's Delegates*, 245.

6. Bernard, *Epistles*, 176.

manifest submission and those who manifest rebellion. Thus, sound doctrine can only lead to ὑποτάσσω, while illegitimate ministry can only encourage behavior that is ἀνυπότακτος, which is behavior that society in general would condemn.

The next infinitive, πειθαρχεῖν, is another instance of paronomasia. The antonym ἀπειθής (1:16) was used in the context of false teachers. Furthermore, the noun ἀρχή occurring in the first part of the sentence is also present in the verb πειθαρχέω. By using paronomasia, the author contrasts the dispositions of the false teachers and believers, perhaps with specific emphasis upon their relationship to authority. Whereas previously the implicit contrasts were being drawn between two opposite groups of teachers, namely legitimate and illegitimate, the focus now falls upon the differences between the illegitimate teachers and legitimate believers. The separation between legitimate and illegitimate groups is hereby sustained.

The expression, ἃ πρὸς πᾶν ἔργον ἀγαθὸν ἑτοίμους εἶναι, but for the infinitive and the adjective, is an exact replication of a previous prepositional phrase: ἃ πρὸς πᾶν ἔργον ἀγαθὸν ἀδόκιμοι (1:16). This is also an instance of implicit contrast between the illegitimate teachers and the legitimate believers. Through implicit contrast, the difference between legitimate and illegitimate is highlighted and maintained. The apostle takes great pains to prevent any blurring of the boundaries between these two opposing sides. Thus, whereas illegitimate teaching renders the one group "worthless for any good work," legitimate teaching makes believers "ready for every good work."

In verse 3, the verb βλασφημεῖν is also a repetition from an earlier occurrence, βλασφημῆται in 2:5. This repetition also constitutes paronomasia. Thus, two things ought not to be spoken evil of, namely God's word and any other person. Interestingly, both instances of this verb appear in close association with the verb ὑποτάσσω. Just as it would be wrong for unbelievers to speak evil of God's word, it would be equally wrong for believers to speak evil of any other person. In fact, evil speaking would put the believer on par with those who speak against the word of God. The adjective μηδείς functions to accentuate the scope of this prohibition, making it applicable to all people—unbelievers and believers alike.

The next two expressions, ἀμάχοι εἶναι (to be uncontentious) and ἐπιεικαί (kind, gentle, tolerant) emphasize the peaceable nature that ought to characterize the believer. It is reminiscent of two synonymous traits associated with elder overseers in 1:7, namely μὴ ὀργίλος (not quick tempered) and μὴ πλήκτης (not pugnacious).

The final characteristic, πραΰτης, is emphasized through alliteration of the consonant π: ἃ πᾶσαν ἐνδεικνυμένους ἃ πραΰτητα ἃ πρὸς ἃ πάντας ἀνθρώπους. The participial clause positively restates the negative μηδένα βλασφηνεῖν and ἀμάχοι εἶναι that occurred earlier. The repetition of the adjective πᾶς reinforces the mandatory and uncompromising nature of these characteristics. This is further enhanced by the pairing of the antonyms πᾶς (all) and μηδείς (none). Thus, any behavior to the contrary is completely unjustifiable—"all gentleness" to "all people," without exceptions.

CONCLUSION

In this section, the dominant rhetorical objective may be summarized as an attempt *to persuade the Cretans of the compulsory treatment of all unbelievers in a manner consistent with sound doctrine*. Paul argues on the basis of the *prior knowledge* of his audience or appeals to the *memory* of his audience to convince them to behave in a socially responsible manner toward authorities and society in general. Verses 1–2 comprise behavior that the audience have known to be commendable—a societal ideal. Implicitly, this appeal seems to be motivated by a concern about the negative influence of illegitimate teaching and the resultant discrediting of the gospel or the Christian movement in Crete. The appeal to memory is a powerful persuasive strategy because it originates from within the individual.

The section begins with the apostolic endorsement of Titus's ministry through the use of an alternative verb in the imperative mode. Several supportive rhetorical techniques include: asyndeton, direct repetition, assonance, and paronomasia. These facilitate intra- and intersectional cohesion. The section also evinces an interesting development in the theme of submission through the paranomastic repetition of the verb ὑποτάσσω. In each of the three occurrences of this verb, there is a different subject and indirect object, and increasing spheres of authoritativeness. This technique ties this section to the rest of the letter and highlights the significance of submission in the Cretan context. The emphasis on submission also calls to mind the false teachers, whose behavior is described as the exact opposite, being ἀνυπότακτος (1:10). This noun is made up of the privative α (without) and ὑποτάσσω.[7] It is also a characteristic that should not manifest in the children of teachers in the church (1:6). This is an instance of the rhetorical technique of paronomasia used here to facilitate a contrast between those who are sound and those who are not. Another striking example of explicit contrast is seen in the direct repetition of the prepositional phrase, πρὸς πᾶν ἔργον ἀγαθόν, which facilitates intersectional cohesion as well as implicit contrast between the illegitimate teachers and the legitimate believers. The ultimate objective is to encourage the Cretans to disassociate themselves from those who seem to encourage behavior considered to be disruptive or subversive. In this way, the apostle launches his strategy to enforce compliance to legitimate teaching by forcing the Cretans to look inside themselves and evaluate whether what he is saying is true or not. But the apostle is not going to leave it there, and in the next section it will be shown how he continues his persuasive strategy through the use of a list of vices.

---

7. Zodhiates, *Dictionary*, s.v. "ἀνυπότακτος."

9

Titus 3:3

Evoking Disgust with Past Sinful Behavior in Order to Reinforce Behavior in the Present That Complies with Sound Doctrine

THE SEVEN VIRTUES IN the previous two verses are counterbalanced in verse 3 by seven vices. The dominant rhetorical objective of this section is to *evoke disgust within the audience toward their past sinful behavior in order to reinforce behavior in the present that complies with sound doctrine*. This interpretation requires some justification in light of the different ways in which commentators treat the list.

Structurally, scholars correctly identify the once/now or ποτέ/ὅτε scheme that characterizes this section, concluding that the purpose of this section is to contrast the old and the new person.[1] Towner and Johnson refer to this as a transition or conversion formula, respectively, the purpose of which is to indicate the transition to the new life.[2] According to Mounce, verse 3 forms part of the theological motivation for the kind of conduct enumerated in the previous section.[3] He maintains that these sins are not directed toward the opponents as much as they are a reflection of the sins of humanity in general. Towner makes the point that the vice list emphasizes the actuality or reality of the change that has

---

1. Collins, *Timothy and Titus*, 358.
2. Towner, *Titus*, 253, 254; Johnson, *Paul's Delegates*, 245.
3. Mounce, *Pastoral Epistles*, 446.

occurred.[4] Latching on to this, Hultgren claims that the reference to a former life in contrast to the present is a literary device employed to make a theological analysis of the presalvific state, without necessarily having any direct bearing on the author or recipients.[5] Fee also believes the list depicts general "human fallenness" and regards 3:3 as the evangelistic motive behind the appeal of 3:1–2.[6] While all of these interpretations are probably correct and highly reasonable, they do not satisfactorily explain the purpose of the list itself. Furthermore, these conclusions are based on premature assumptions about the applicability of these vices to the stated recipients. Scholars are hesitant to apply the vices listed here to those whom the apostle identifies as "we." Thus, Quinn avers that these lists are "not biographical, much less autobiographical" and "the items of this vice catalogue are not vices as such; they are adjectival of persons."[7] While there may be a modicum of truth in this comment, it downplays what the text intends to communicate about the recipients and the purpose behind the list. In all fairness to Quinn, he does eventually, in his explanation for the abrupt conclusion of verse 3, allude to the function of these lists as "bring[ing] the reader up short."[8] Bernard captures the intent of this verse as indicated by his chapter heading: "No Reason for Pride."[9] Unfortunately he does not elaborate upon this in the rest of his commentary. In a single sentence, Simpson succinctly expresses the intention of the list, namely "to inspire disgust."[10] The "affective" function of these lists, particularly that of the vice list, is a notion that most commentators seem not to appreciate fully. These lists were intended to affect the recipients. The graphic description of the vices, which fills even a modern audience with disgust, supports such an interpretation. The overarching rhetorical objective in 3:3 is to fill the audience with disgust, to show them up. Why? The candor of the apostle is only justifiable if he is enforcing compliance to sound doctrine.

Most modern commentators provide more than adequate explanations for the vocabulary that comprises verse 3 and may be consulted

4. Towner, *Goal*, 253.
5. Hultgren, *Timothy, Titus*, 168.
6. Fee, *Titus*, 202.
7. Quinn, *Letter to Titus*, 200.
8. Ibid., 208.
9. Bernard, *Epistles*, 177.
10. Simpson, *Greek Text*, 114.

for that purpose. My focus involves highlighting some of the rhetorical techniques that tie this section into a coherent unit. These include alliteration and rhyme, chiasmus, inclusive language, implicit contrast, and "emphatic pairing."

Paul uses the conjunction γάρ rhetorically (2:11) to emphasize the relationship between the present section and the previous one. The enclitic particle ποτέ anticipates the follow-up to this verse with its parallel particle in the next verse, namely ὅτε, to form what scholars identify as a transition or conversion formula.[11] Another rhetorical technique occurs in the use of the verb ἦμεν in the first person plural, with the personal pronoun, ἡμεῖς. The purpose is clearly to emphasize inclusiveness and to facilitate identification between the apostle, Titus, and the Cretan believers. Quinn believes this expresses a relational purpose while Mounce believes it is emphatic to accentuate the contrast between the past and present life.[12] The latter may be a secondary objective, but its primary objective must certainly be the facilitation of a relationship with the emphasis upon the "rhetorical identification with his audience."[13] Paul's relationship with the audience softens the harshness of the list by presenting Paul as an insider and not as a judge speaking from a sanctimonious height. Conversely, it conveys the humility of the apostle to establish apostolic pathos. According to Hendriksen, "it causes the reader (Titus) and the hearers (the Cretan believers when the letter is read to them) to feel that the writer is standing on common ground with them and understands them."[14] This interpretation is in line with the pattern that has characterized the discourse thus far. Paul argues from the basis of *identification with his audience* in order to enforce compliance to the required behavioral conduct.

Collins and Quinn offer insightful comments with reference to the rhetorical arrangement of this verse.[15] The opening two vices, ἀνόητος and ἀπειθής, both contain alpha privatives. The latter word is an instance of paronomasia and is used for emphasis. It is a direct repetition of the word that appears in 1:16, which describes the false teachers. It is also the antonym of the virtue that appears in 3:1. The effect of this word can

---

11. Towner, *Goal*, 253; Johnson, *Paul's Delegates*, 245.
12. Quinn, *Letter to Titus*, 201; Mounce, *Pastoral Epistles*, 446.
13. Johnson, *Paul's Delegates*, 247.
14. Hendriksen, *Timothy and Titus*, 387.
15. Collins, *Epistle to Titus*, 358; Quinn, *Letter to Titus*, 201.

best be visualized when we outline the order in which it appears in the discourse:

1. ἀπειθής: negative, false teachers in the present (1:16)
2. πειθαρχεῖν: positive, believers in the present (3:1)
3. ἀπειθής: negative, believers in the past (3:3)

The persuasive effect of this technique is compelling: any manifestation of being ἀπειθής is a step backward, a step into the past, a step into fellowship with the false teachers.

The paronomasia, combined with the double negative, in the form of two alpha privatives, highlights the heinous nature of disobedience, by linking it with the vilification section, more specifically, a section where a profession to know God is cancelled out by ethical conduct that translates into a denial of God. The present vice list is therefore a graphic picture of behavior that demonstrates an absence of the knowledge of God. In other words, Paul is saying, "We also were like 'them.' " The use of this shame list constitutes what I term *self-vilification*, which serves to induce disgust within the hearers. By forcing them to remember their past, especially the shamefulness thereof, the overarching rhetorical objective of compliance to the sound teaching is compellingly reinforced.

Quinn is particularly helpful when he demonstrates how, through rhyming endings (assonance) in –οι, several items on the list are linked.[16] Thus, ἀνόητοι is linked with the third word, πλανώμενοι, and the sixth, στυγητοί. The list evinces a combination of asyndeton and syndetic pairing. The conjunction, καί, appears very strategically within the two participial phrases of the sentence: δουλεύοντες ἐπιθυμίαις καί ἡδοναῖς ποικίλαις ἐν κακίᾳ καί φθόνῳ διάγοντες. Quinn is perhaps correct when he identifies this as the "central chiasmus" of the section.[17] Moreover, he shows how the assonated sounds encircle the central chiasmus:

| A—δουλεύοντες | B—ἐπιθυμίαις καί ἡδοναῖς ποικίλαις |
| B*—ἐν κακίᾳ καί φθόνῳ | A*—διάγοντες |

This chiasmus is introduced and concluded by the alliteration and rhyme of δουλεύοντες . . . διάγοντες.[18] The rhetorical function of the

16. Quinn, *Letter to Titus*, 201.
17. Ibid.
18. Ibid., 202.

chiasm is to emphasize how servitude to vice (δουλεύοντες) becomes a manner of life (διάγοντες). The verb δουλεύω is furthermore an instance of paronomasia. It has been preceded by the noun δοῦλος in both plural (2:9) and singular (1:1) form. Its use, however, in this present context, is a development of the previous two occasions in that it now functions in a metaphorical sense. The two earlier instances of the theme of slavery were communicated in a positive light, while the present one is presented as negative. Paronomasia and the metaphorical nuance of slavery thus highlight the negative side of enslavement. True freedom is therefore not freedom from an earthly or divine master, but rather from ἐπιθυμίαις καὶ ἡδοναῖς ποικίλαις, and ἐν κακίᾳ καὶ φθόνῳ διάγοντες. In other words, the real slaves are not those who serve earthly masters, but those who serve sin. Interestingly, the apostle, by using the first-person plural pronoun, presents himself as one who is presently a slave of God (1:1), and as one who was previously (ποτέ) a slave of sin (3:3).

Scholars are keen to interpret the vice list as follows: we were not really much better than other people; "hence let us not be too hard on the people who are still in that condition, but let us strive by godly conduct to win them for Christ."[19] Such an interpretation unfortunately ignores the key concern of this discourse, namely, the supremacy, efficacy, and necessity of sound teaching, and hence the urgency of compliance to sound teaching. The evangelistic efficacy of the gospel follows as a result of the believers' compliance and embracing, through the totality of their lives, of legitimate teaching. The Cretans are not yet at the place where they have grasped or demonstrated that they have grasped the necessity for legitimate teaching. Instead, there is reason to believe that they are allowing themselves to come under the influence of illegitimate teachers and their teaching, resulting in conduct that places the integrity of God's word or legitimate teaching at risk. These two lists present them with an opportunity to evaluate their pre- and postconversion behavior. It holds before them two kinds of behavior that are mutually exclusive. The overall rhetorical impact of this section is to emphasize the utter unworthiness of Paul, Titus, the Cretan believers, and the rest of humanity.

---

19. Hendriksen, *Timothy and Titus*, 389.

CONCLUSION

The dominant rhetorical objective of the vice list in verse 3 is *to evoke disgust at past sinful behavior, in order to reinforce behavior in the present that complies with sound doctrine*. It has been shown how scholars all too often gloss over this section by (a) interpreting it exclusively from an evangelistic perspective and (b) portraying it as primarily a picture of human sinfulness. The section is applicable firstly to the Cretans, Paul, and Titus, and then to the rest of humanity.

The section evinces what I refer to as *self-vilification*. The purpose of the shame list is to evoke disgust within the hearers with a concomitant sense of worthlessness. Through the once/now or ποτέ/ὅτε scheme, which serves as a transitional device, the author is anticipating the event that made the difference in his audience, something they would only appreciate once they've come to terms with their own unworthiness.

Intrasectional coherence is achieved through rhetorical techniques like alliteration and rhyme, chiasmus, inclusive language, implicit contrast, and "emphatic pairing." Intersectional coherence is achieved through the use of the conjunction γάρ, along with paronomasia and repetition, particularly of the following words: ἀπειθεῖς and δουλεύοντες. The latter word is also used in a metaphorical way as opposed to its "normal" meaning in the rest of the letter. We also have in this section the simultaneous use of asyndeton and syndeton, with the latter in a structure referred to as syndetic pairing. All of these are emphatic and used to facilitate coherence within the discourse. The apostle argues from the basis of *identification with his audience* in order to achieve his objective of engendering a compliant attitude. This technique provides the apostle with a platform from which to address his audience, effectively reinforcing his authority over or right to address them with such candor.

10

Titus 3:4–7

Persuading the Cretans that Displaying Good Works to Those Considered Undeserving Conforms to the Divine Example

IN THIS SECTION, PAUL's dominant rhetorical objective is to persuade the Cretans that displaying good works to those considered undeserving demonstrates conformity to the divine example. In order to achieve this objective, Paul structures his argument by appealing to the divine example. To this extent, he adapts traditional material to remind his audience of God's salvific intervention. The highly theological nature of this section continues to evoke much discussion and debate. A rhetorical analysis of this passage necessitates an evaluation of how scholars tend to treat it. It will become clear how some scholars have already suggested the interpretation adopted in this study without actually developing it far enough.

Some general observations on this passage must precede the evaluation of academic treatment of this passage. Verses 4–7 constitute a single sentence in the original. Salvation is clearly the main focus of the sentence as indicated by the main verb and direct object, ἔσωσεν ἡμᾶς. The rest of verse 5 concisely expresses, according to Fee, "the *basis* (his mercy), the *what* (new birth, renewal, justified), the *means* (by the Holy Spirit, 'by his [Christ's] grace'), and the *goal* (the hope of eternal life) of salvation."[1] Expressions like the "Gospel in a nutshell,"[2] the "essence of the gospel"[3] or "the gospel summarized in a highly condensed form"[4] confirm that scholars recognize the essential content of this sentence.

Scholarly treatment of this passage is characterized by a debate that is both intense and technical. One area that continues to attract discussion involves the character and delineation of the section. In regard to the former, scholars cannot decide whether this passage is a hymn,[5] a liturgical formula, a creedal formula,[6] or a baptismal prayer or act of praise.[7] With regard to the latter, Hanson adopts a source-critical approach by arguing for the existence of a common or original source shared by the authors of the Letter to Titus, 1 Peter, and Ephesians.[8]

Among academics, this passage is treated as a hymn—an insistence based primarily on typological and, more importantly, textual considerations, although not all agree with this proposal.[9] Next, scholars are divided on the delineation of the formula. An offshoot from the authenticity debate, it relates to the differentiation made between traditional

1. Fee, *Titus*, 203.
2. Simpson, *Greek Text*, 115.
3. Demarest, *Timothy, Titus*, 326.
4. Oden, *Timothy and Titus*, 36.
5. Guthrie, *Pastoral Epistles*, 204; Karris, *Symphony*, 127.
6. Mounce, *Pastoral Epistles*, 440; Fee, *Titus*, 203.
7. Hanson, *Studies*, 95.
8. Ibid., 83, 86, 90, 95, 96.
9. Karris, *Symphony*, 127, insists that it "is indeed a hymn" arguing that the section conforms to six of Markus Barth's eleven "objective" criteria "for detecting the existence of hymns in the New Testament." Although he refers to six, he only lists the following five: (1) The passage uses verbs as aorist participles in relative clauses and in consecutive clauses (criterion 3). (2) Those who benefit from God's mighty acts speak in the first person plural (criterion 4). (3) There are unique words present (criterion 6). (4) The section has artistic structure—"parallelism" (criterion 8). (5) The content of a given passage interrupts the context (criterion 11). Karris bases his typological considerations on the fact that this section is indented by the editors of the NASB and the twenty-seventh edition of *Novum Testamentum Graece* (*Symphony*, 127, 128). Karris believes that it would not be indented if it was not considered poetic or hymnic. He also cites Ralph Martin, a scholar of hymns who includes Titus 3:4–7 as part of the "sacramental" hymns.

Mounce, *Pastoral Epistles*, 440, disagrees with Karris, because the suggested hymnic structure is disrupted by the unusual placement of ἔσωσεν ἡμᾶς. Furthermore, there are other criteria suggestive of a creed rather than a hymn. These include the use of plural pronouns and a purpose clause in verse 7 rather than an indicative. According to Fee, *Titus*, 203, the sentence "altogether lacks the poetic elements of a hymn."

material and Pauline additions. With regard to traditional material, various possibilities are posited as traditional sections: verses 3–7, 5b–6, and 5–7. The prevailing theory is to regard verses 4–7 as traditional, with verse 3 viewed as an addition.[10] Still, the matter remains moot, since "it is virtually impossible to differentiate between traditional and Pauline material with any degree of certainty."[11]

Another area of debate relates to the meaning of the word λουτρόν and its relationship to what follows in the rest of the sentence. Four translations are possible: cleansing from sin, baptism, baptism of the Spirit, and physically bathing in a laver or bath. Oden follows the classical view that regards baptism as the bath of the new birth.[12] Simpson takes issue with the Roman Catholic or sacramental interpretation of this sentence that interprets διὰ λουτροῦ as denoting the material apparatus of baptism, namely the laver or bath.[13] He argues that the word refers to baptism and simply means "washing." Hendriksen supports this interpretation, adding that "the washing referred to is wholly spiritual."[14] Karris disagrees, insisting that the word refers to "a bath," which was a "ubiquitous Roman institution" used for recreation and ablution purposes by all citizens.[15] The image of the bath would strike a chord with the audience of this letter rather than the "dominant image" of baptism in our modern day Christian language, although some scholars prefer not to interpret the word in a strict baptismal sense, arguing instead that the word is a metaphor for inner or spiritual "cleansing."[16] On the other end of the spectrum, there is Hultgren, who interprets διὰ λουτροῦ παλιγγενεσίας καὶ ἀνακαινώσεως πνεύματος ἁγίου as a reference to baptismal regeneration in which "God saves through baptism."[17] Alternatively it describes spiritual baptism and emphasizes the "salvation-historical orientation of the passage."[18]

10. Knight, *Faithful Sayings*, 81; Mounce, *Pastoral Epistles*, 440.
11. Mounce, *Pastoral Epistles*, 441.
12. Oden, *Timothy and Titus*, 37.
13. Simpson, *Greek Text*, 115–16.
14. Hendriksen, *Timothy and Titus*, 391.
15. Karris, *Symphony*, 135.
16. See Mounce, *Pastoral Epistles*, 439, who maintains, "It is possible for the New Testament to use the imagery of cleansing without any reference to baptism." See also Fee, *Titus*, 204–5.
17. Hultgren, *Timothy, Titus*, 169.
18. Towner, *Goal*, 115, 117.

A related area of debate focuses on the collection of genitives that follow the preposition διά. Fee's helpfully succinct summary of the debate, which I paraphrase below, must suffice:[19]

1. The word λουτροῦ refers to conversion (or baptism) and ἀνακαινώσεως to the coming of the Spirit. Both are dependent upon διά and refer to *two distinct* realities. Thus, "through the 'washing' found in rebirth and through the renewal that comes with the gift of the Spirit." However, the narrow proximity in meaning between the words παλιγγενεσίας and ἀνακαινώσεως weakens this interpretation since it would necessitate an additional διά to make this meaning clear. Interestingly, this is the interpretation propounded by Mounce, who puts forth the following arguments in defense of his position: (a) Regeneration and renewal, though contemporaneous events, are none the less distinct realities; (b) renewal is never described as a washing, therefore ἀνακαινώσεως cannot be said to modify λουτροῦ; (c) if the imagery of washing suggests a "once-and-for-all" cleansing and renewal refers to the believer's initial renewal, then we find in the words παλιγγενεσίας and ἀνακαινώσεως a description of the singular conversion event from a dual perspective; (d) stylistically, the dependence upon διά maintains a better parallelism; (e) Paul characteristically omits the second preposition (διά) in a construction where a preposition governs a series of phrases connected by καί; (f) the absence of an additional article such as τοῦ or preposition such as ὑπό preceding πνεύματος ἁγίου enhances its proximity to ἀνακαινώσεως. The additional article or preposition would have brought παλιγγενεσίας and ἀνακαινώσεως closer together while its absence appears to corroborate the notion that the two are separate; (g) the dependence of the four genitives upon the preposition διά eliminates interpreting the sentence as teaching the doctrine of justification by baptism.[20] He concludes that "Paul is describing one event, not two."[21] Unanimity about the interpretation of the genitival string remains remote.[22]

19. Fee, *Titus*, 204–5.
20. Mounce, *Pastoral Epistles*, 442–43.
21. Ibid., 443.
22. Mounce, *Pastoral Epistles*, 442, is prepared to acknowledge "[i]t is difficult to decide between the two, and in many cases the distinctions are not that significant." He

2. The word λουτροῦ refers exclusively to baptism, and the two genitives παλιγγενεσίας and ἀνακαινώσεως, which are effected by the Holy Spirit, depend upon it. Thus, the phrase could be translated as "through the regenerating and renewing work of baptism effected by the Holy Spirit." The terms therefore, function either synonymously or complimentarily. While this interpretation has much that commends it, it nevertheless tends to emphasize baptism in a manner that stretches the present context.

3. The word λουτροῦ is a metaphor for spiritual cleansing and not a synonym for baptism. It emphasizes the cleansing, regenerative work of the Holy Spirit and is translatable as "through the *washing* by the Holy Spirit that brings rebirth and renewal." This view conforms to Pauline theology concerning the centrality of the Holy Spirit[23] for Christian existence and is seemingly confirmed by the emphasis maintained in the sentence.

In summary, the influence of the authenticity debate is clearly felt in the analysis of the sentence. A definite correspondence exists between the lack of consent around the extent and delineation of the passage and the degree to which scholars regard portions of the sentence or passage as authentically Pauline or not. The same holds for the interpretation of the word λουτρόν. Apart from textual considerations, continuity or discontinuity with Pauline theology significantly affects the interpretation of this word. The debate around the nature of the passage is less influenced by the authenticity issue. The above discussion represents the primary areas of contention in the translation and analysis of this passage. It would be remiss to highlight the areas of disagreement, while ignoring what scholars generally agree upon in regard to this section.

There is widespread consensus around the content of the sentence. Commentators generally agree about the soteriological nature, Trinitarian

---

is joined in this regard by Bernard, *Epistles*, 178, who admits that "both (1) and (2) are admissible in grammar."

23. Fee, *Titus*, 205, believes that παλιγγενεσίας and ἀνακαινώσεως are "twin metaphors for the same spiritual reality—the re-creating work of the Holy Spirit in the believer's life."

character, and doctrinal congruence of this passage with 2:11–15.[24] The themes of divine grace and salvation have also not gone unnoticed.[25]

These and every interpretation given by scholars has some degree of legitimacy or represents an accurate interpretation of an aspect of the sentence. However, regarding the full import of what the apostle is communicating, room exists for additional contributions, especially in light of the context of the entire letter thus far.

The shortcomings surrounding scholarly discussions of this section relate to scholars' analysis of the passage within the context of the letter itself. Many interpret the passage within the context of Pauline theology, attempting to reconcile their interpretation with what can be found elsewhere, either extrabiblically or in the rest of the New Testament. For example, Mounce, in his otherwise excellent commentary, does not see this section as contributing anything new to the apostle's argument, observing that "Titus 3:1–11 is a repetition of 2:1–14."[26] Perhaps I am being overly critical of an unfortunate choice in vocabulary, but as my analysis will show, there is a significant development in this part of the argument, more than a mere repetition of what is said earlier. Likewise, Oden is content to classify this section as the epitome of "the word of justification by grace."[27] True, the passage touches on justification by grace, but to imply that it does so exclusively or that this constitutes the primary function of this section cannot be entirely justified.

Others simply fail to relate this section to the rest of the letter, except for pointing out obvious linguistic correspondences. Collins, for example, is of the opinion that this section is simply a return to the epiphany motive.[28] While he is not altogether incorrect, there is more to this passage than simply a thematic revisit of the "saving appearance of Jesus Christ,

---

24. Mounce, *Pastoral Epistles*, 450; Karris, *Symphony*, 129; Towner, *Titus*, 258; Quinn, *Letter to Titus*, 212; Oden, *Timothy and Titus*, 37; Fee, *Titus*, 206; Hendriksen, *Timothy and Titus*, 392; Van Neste, "Message," 25.

25. See Demarest, *Timothy, Titus*, 328: "Precisely at the point where God has every right to express his judgment of us, he chooses instead to meet us with kindness and love." See also Simpson, *Greek Text*, 115: "Salvation by grace stands forth in clearest relief in the language employed, which effectually excludes all glory on man's part and denies to any stock of good works amassed by any sinner a 'merit of congruity' drawing forth the riches of divine mercy."

26. Mounce, *Pastoral Epistles*, 443, 455.

27. Oden, *Timothy and Titus*, 35.

28. Collins, *Timothy and Titus*, 359.

our Savior." In fact, the primary focus of scholarly works consulted is on the nature of the sentence, specifically its origin as a baptismal hymn or creed. Other commentators appear to get lost in linguistic analyses and etymological studies, all of which are valid and render valuable insights into the vocabulary, but unfortunately fail to adequately relate the passage to its immediate and extended contexts.

The tendency to make baptism and salvation the foci of the passage is a major criticism. Thus, scholars approach the text with a preconceived notion of, for example, baptism or baptismal regeneration, utterly disregarding the recorded order of the sentence. In regard to the latter, some (correctly) point out the main verb of the sentence and make that the starting point of their interpretation. Unfortunately, that is not the best way to approach the text. A better approach would be to deal with the structure of the sentence in the way it has been recorded, in order to appreciate the different syntactical relationships within the sentence and the section at large. The interpretative shortcomings apparently relate to the grinding of theological axes and vocabulary analyses instead of appreciating the sentence as it stands and seeking more adequate explanations for the unusual nature of the sentence structure. In this regard, the interpretative options of George Knight III and Jerome Quinn prove helpful.

The former draws attention to the second word in verse 4, namely δέ, which captures the essence of this passage and relates it to the preceding verses, namely 1–3.[29] Contrasts are clearly in view; the characteristics of God and the characteristics of believers' past condition: "This attitude of God is contrasted with Christians' past attitude (verse 3) so that no one less than God the merciful Savior can be the *norm* for exhorting Christians 'to be gentle, showing all meekness toward all people' (verse 2), since God showed to the Christians his 'kindness and love toward mankind' when they were as 'all people' are now."[30] The normative role of the divine example is a key aspect in our understanding of this sentence. Unfortunately, Knight neither takes this up again in the rest his analysis nor does he relate it to the argument in the earlier part of the letter.

Quinn's summary of this sentence evinces a better appreciation for the rhetorical nuance of the sentence. In his own words:

---

29. Knight, *Pastoral Epistles*, 338.
30. Ibid., 338. Emphasis added.

> Jews were devoted to the God who loved humankind; they could not reasonably hate what their God loved. . . . Jesus, the Savior, was the visible, historical revelation of God's *philanthrōpia* to all human beings. That vision of the baptismal profession became in its turn the antithesis to the vicious existence that converts from extremist Jewish sects had once led. They had formerly been "detested, hating one another." Now, in faith, they have seen "the humane munificence of our savior, God . . . revealed." *They have no longer any basis for hating those whom God, their Father and savior, has loved.*[31]

This comparative-contrastive dimension best explains the function of this unusual sentence. The apostle has not abandoned his dominant rhetorical objective, namely to enforce compliance to sound doctrine. Instead, he takes his argument a notch higher in this final of three strategic, though unusually long sentences, occurring here, in 1:1–4 and in 2:11–14. Each of these three long sentences forms a strategic part of the rhetorical strategy of the author. He thus tends to use these sentences to communicate highly concentrated theology. Each sentence contains shared knowledge or traditional material apparently known to the recipients. The present sentence is therefore also a strategically placed rhetorical technique. After shaming the believers through *self-vilification* in the opening verses of this chapter, the apostle does not relent. The employment of the ποτὲ/ὅτε formula serves to connect this sentence with the previous section. Thus, the argument based on prior knowledge is implicitly perpetuated in this section. The believers must be reminded about good conduct (vv. 1–2), about what they were (v. 3), and now the apostle reminds them of what God did while they were unworthy of God's beneficence. Paul is enforcing compliance to sound doctrine arguing now on the basis of *the power of the divine example*. Believers' past negative conduct, discussed in verse 3, is juxtaposed with the positive attitude of God in the opening description of verse 4. The ποτὲ-ὅτε formula emphasizes this contrast. Thus, when believers are instructed to manifest the positive behavior of 3:1–2 to outsiders, lack of compliance will put them at variance not with other people, but with God. Furthermore, this argument is based on transcendent conduct. When believers manifest these attitudes, their behavior transcends common decency or what is expected from good citizens. Their conduct testifies

---

31. Quinn, *Letter to Titus*, 215. Emphasis added.

about something extraordinary that has happened to them, namely the way God treated them! This is certainly a powerful line of reasoning—highly convincing and persuasive. A schematic presentation of the argument will demonstrate the careful reasoning in which the contrasts between the divine and human actions are accentuated:

a. Present: believers manifesting positive behavior (3:1–2)

b. Past: believers manifesting negative behavior (3:3)

c. Past: God manifesting positive behavior (3:4–7)

d. Present: believers manifesting positive behavior (3:8)

Most scholars recognize the temporal aspects of this sentence (v. 3–7), particularly the believers' past conduct and the attitude and intervention of the divine in the past but are less appreciative of the rhetorical intent and function behind these shifts in temporal perspectives.

The lack of unanimity among scholars in identifying or categorizing this section prohibits any dogmatic notions about the nature of the section. The most that can be said is that this section contains elements of traditional material. Attempts to classify it as either a hymn or creed cloud the rhetorical intent behind the sentence. For the purposes of this study, I advocate categorizing this sentence as constituting *shared knowledge* and hence as forming part of the overall rhetorical intent of the passage. Paul is adapting the traditional material in a manner that draws attention to the salvific activity of the triune God and not primarily to present a comprehensive theological treatise. He wishes instead to accentuate the lavishness of the divine condescension toward people who did not deserve it. The rich and distinct theological flavor is empathic, drawing attention to and highlighting the benevolent action of the divine. In fact, if the structure of the sentence is appreciated, it provides a clearer indication of the apostolic intent of this sentence.

This section is inspired by the rhetorical objective of motivating compliance to sound doctrine. If someone dared to ask Titus, "Why must I show kindness to these unsaved Cretans?" the answer would be, "Look at what you were and look at how God treated you." Furthermore, there also appears to be a polemical intention behind this section. The false teaching seems to have encouraged isolationist tendencies, even hostility toward pagan neighbors, who appear to have been branded as unworthy to associate with. This kind of thinking is confronted head on by the argument of the apostle in this section.

Most commentators provide elaborate and helpful vocabulary studies of this sentence and may be consulted for further information. Priority should instead be given to sentence order rather than to the unusual vocabulary, since "it is the sentences which he arranges in such a way as to give his words special force and emphasis."[32] Prominent rhetorical features in this section include syndeton, implicit contrast, repetition, and paronomasia. Other features include emotive or anthropopathic, highly theological, inclusive language.

In earlier sections, implicit contrasts are drawn primarily on the human level, whereas in the present situation the contrast takes on a different dimension. The χρηστότης and φιλανθρωπία of God are contrasted with the unworthy condition of believers in their preconversion state (v. 3). This is borne out by the ποτὲ/ὅτε construction, which links the two sentences. The words χρηστότης and φιλανθρωπία are examples of the rhetorical technique called anthropopathism, so entitled because of the approximation of human emotions to the divine. The rhetorical objective of this strategy is twofold. First, it presents God in a manner that people can identify with; it personalizes God. Secondly, it emphasizes the stark contrast between the divine attitude and those human qualities listed in 3:3 as well as those negative qualities referred to with respect to false teachers and their followers (1:10-12, 15-16). Interestingly, this vocabulary combination appears extrabiblically with reference to certain Roman emperors, individuals, and other ancient rulers.[33]

The expression ἡ χρηστότης καὶ ἡ φιλανθρωπία is an example of syndeton. Classen points out the "asyndetic enumeration" of the Cretans' past behavior (3:3), here contrasted with the *syndetonic enumeration* of the divine attitude.[34] The use of asyndeton and syndeton serves to accentuate the contrast between the opposing attitudes while magnifying the distinctiveness of the divine beneficence. Another helpful enumeration by Classen is the pairing of significant concepts that are evident in this sentence: "ἡ χρηστότης καὶ ἡ φιλανθρωπία, ἔργα τὰ ἐν δικαιοσύνῃ ἃ ἐποιήσαμεν ἡμεῖς/τὸ αὐτοῦ ἔλεος /, λουτρὸν παλιγγενεσίας καὶ ἀνακαινώσεως πνεύματος ἁγίου."[35] The notion of contrast between the divine and human is consistently emphasized in this brilliant sentence; reinforced by

32. Classen, *Rhetorical Criticism*, 61.
33. Collins, *Timothy and Titus*, 361-62.
34. Classen, *Rhetorical Criticism*, 60.
35. Ibid., 61.

the antithesis that Classen highlights. The primary objective does not involve presenting a fully orbed Pauline theological treatise. This is an important observation since many scholars appear to get sidetracked precisely at this point: they want to prove or disprove whether this sentence correctly reflects authentic Pauline theology. The author is simply exalting the excellence of the divine example over against the poverty of the preconversion human condition. If it was simply a matter of conveying knowledge, i.e., theology, then there is much that the apostle is *not* saying. However, the original hearers would have *heard* this sentence in a manner of seconds.[36] They would not have heard detailed information per se but rather a rhetorical intention that would force them to compare themselves with none other than God. The audacity of the statement is calculated. Tolmie makes this comment about provocative sentences: "[a] provocative utterance is not arrived at slowly by a careful process of thought. It is flung out in the heat of debate—and the hearer in the sentence is left to consider in what sense or senses it is true."[37] Therefore, in the debate surrounding the nature of the discourse, the adamancy to categorize the sentences as either a creed or a hymn proves rather fruitless. It is unquestionable that the sentence resembles traditional aspects. The most that can be maintained is that the apostle has modified this traditional material to serve a rhetorical purpose, namely to emphasize the exemplary nature of the divine example. The net effect of this customization of traditional material is that the audience is confronted with a choice: either follow inferior teaching modeled by inferior examples or follow sound teaching and a superior example—neither Paul, nor Titus, but God. The ultimate consequence of sound teaching is to make the attitude of the adherent thereof conform to that of God.

Other rhetorical strategies include inclusive language, repetition, antithesis, and theological vocabulary. This section contains a high concentration of inclusive language in pronoun and verbal forms:

1. τοῦ σωτῆρος ἡμῶν θεου (v. 4)
2. ἐποιήσαμεν ἡμεῖς (v. 5)
3. ἔσωσεν ἡμᾶς (v. 5)
4. οὗ ἐξέχεεν ἐφ' ἡμᾶς (v. 6)

---

36. See Tolmie, *Persuading the Galatians*, 132.
37. Ibid.

5. Ἰησοῦ Χριστοῦ τοῦ σωτῆρος ἡμῶν (v. 6)

6. γενηθῶμεν (v. 6)

In verse 5, the pronoun functions emphatically since the verb ἐποιήσαμεν already contains the first person plural ending. The pronoun highlights the antithesis between divine grace and human works: οὐκ ἐξ ἔργων τῶν ἐν δικαιοσύνῃ ἃ ἐποιησαμεν ἡμεῖς (works) ἀλλὰ κατὰ τὸ αὐτοῦ ἔλεος (grace) ἔσωσεν ἡμᾶς. There seems to be a polemical intent behind this sentence, particularly the negation concerning a "work's righteousness." It is probable that the false teaching emphasized a belief in a "work's righteousness" or that there was a leniency toward such a teaching among the Cretan believers, hence the strong negation on the part of the apostle. If we accept the notion that this sentence constitutes some form of tradition or shared knowledge, it would underscore the polemical nuance of the sentence. It makes sense rhetorically to counter any doctrinal aberrance by reciting doctrine already known to the believers.

The sentence ὅτε δὲ ἡ χρηστότης καὶ ἡ φιλανθρωπία ἐπεφάνη τοῦ σωτῆρος ἡμῶν θεοῦ (v. 4) is parallel to that of 2:11. These two sentences share several commonalities. For example, they contain the same verb in the aorist, namely ἐπιφαίνω. In 2:11, it is ἡ χάρις τοῦ θεοῦ that appeared. In 3:4, it is the manifestation of ἡ χρηστότης and ἡ φιλανθρωπία . . . τοῦ . . . θεοῦ that is in the spotlight. The use of this verb, together with the synonymous verb in 1:3, φανερόω, conveys the notion of accessibility or the absence of secrecy. God has done everything openly and publicly. There are no secrets; whether it is a question of the source of Paul's authority to teach (1:3) or the contents of sound doctrine (2:11–12) or the nature of the divine beneficence (3:4), it is all known. The employment of this verb seems to counter any notions of secrecy perhaps taught by the false teachers.

Paronomasia is seen in the occurrence of the noun σωτήρ and adjective σωτήριος found respectively in 3:4 and 2:11. Also, both sentences contain the expression τοῦ . . . θεοῦ. In 2:11, it is divine grace that appeared, while in 3:4 it is divine kindness and love for humankind. The presence of the third-person singular verb ἐπεφάνη has lead some scholars to view the expression χρηστότης καὶ ἡ φιλανθρωπία as conveying a single concept, namely the divine attitude.[38] The paronomasia and parallel expressions facilitate intertextual coherence between the

---

38. Knight, *Pastoral Epistles*, 338; Hendriksen, *Timothy and Titus*, 389.

above respective sections. Coherence extends to the rest of the letter, specifically the opening verses of this letter, by an interesting theological exchange of titles between God and Jesus Christ. In 1:3–4, we find the following references to God and Jesus Christ:

a. τοῦ σωτῆρος ἡμῶν θεοῦ (1:3)

b. Χριστοῦ Ἰησοῦ τοῦ σωτῆρος ἡμῶν (1:4)

In 3:4 and 3:6, the exact references are repeated:

c. τοῦ σωτῆρος ἡμῶν θεοῦ (3:4)

d. Ἰησοῦ Χριστοῦ τοῦ σωτῆρος ἡμῶν (3:6)

In both of the above instances, the references form a chiasm. Interestingly, in 2:13 all of the above vocabulary appears again. Only this time, it refers exclusively to Jesus Christ who is called both our God and Savior: (ἐπιφάνειαν τῆς δόξης τοῦ μεγάλου) θεοῦ καὶ σωτῆρος ἡμῶν Ἰησοῦ Χριστοῦ.

Note in the above sentence the presence of the noun form (ἐπιφάνεια), which derives from the verb ἐπιφαίνω. This makes the occurrence of the verb, in 3:5, another instance of paronomasia. These direct repetitions bind the letter into a coherent unit that evinces development of the Christological motif. Viewed holistically, the following outline demonstrates the Christological progression within the letter:

a. 1:3—God our Savior (past)

b. 1:4—(God our Father) Christ Jesus our Savior (present)

c. 2:13—our (great) God and Savior Jesus Christ (future)

d. 3:4—God our Savior (past)

e. 3:6—Jesus Christ our Savior (past)

It is only in 1:1, 1:4, and 2:13 that the words *God* and *Jesus Christ* or *Christ Jesus* occur together. In the first two instances, they refer to two separate persons, whereas in the last instance a single person is in view. Thus, in the presentation of Jesus Christ, there is progression. Furthermore, it is interesting to note from the above scheme the time referents associated with these titles. The future appearance of Jesus Christ as God and Savior appears to be a central theme in the letter. This outline confirms the scholarly consensus surrounding the soteriological character of the letter.

In verse 5, the contrast between the divine and human attitudes is also highlighted through assonance of the ε vowel in the nouns ἔργων and ἔλεος, as well as in the verbs ἐποιήσαμεν and ἔσωσεν. Furthermore, the order in which the audience would have heard the divine and human actions described also accentuates the differences:

1. God (v. 4): ἡ χρηστότης καὶ ἡ φιλανθρωπία
2. Human (v. 5): ἔργων τῶν ἐν δικαιοσύνῃ
3. God (v. 5): ἔλεος

The aural impact is overwhelming in this section because God is presented as the sole actor with humanity at the receiving end of divine benevolence: God saved the saints (ἔσωσεν) (v. 5) and poured out the Spirit richly (ἐξέχεεν ἐφ' ἡμᾶς πλουσίως) (v. 6) upon them. The adverb πλουσίως reiterates the generous nature of divine salvation: God was not parsimonious when God acted. Thus, the Cretans are without excuse, having no reason to boast or to avoid compliance to sound doctrine. Any action contrary to that stipulated in 3:1-2 would amount to flagrant disobedience or serve as proof that they do not belong to the divine family (see 1:4). To disobey, in the light of such divine lavishness, would be unthinkable to a true believer. The basis of their being part of the divine family lies entirely outside of themselves: they were saved not from ἔργων τῶν ἐν δικαιοσύνῃ but κατὰ τὸ αὐτοῦ ἔλεος. The careful and deliberate structuring of the argument suggests an embedded polemic against a doctrine of works righteousness or salvation by human effort, particularly by observing the law.[39]

The repetition of the noun ἔργον, while facilitating coherence throughout the text, recalls previous appearances of the word. These are as follows:

1. τοῖς δὲ ἔργοις ἀρνοῦνται (1:16)
2. πρὸς πᾶν ἔργον ἀγαθὸν ἀδόκιμοι (1:16)
3. καλῶν ἔργων (2:7)
4. ζηλωτὴν καλῶν ἔργων (2:14)
5. ἔργον ἀγαθόν (3:1)
6. οὐκ ἐξ ἔργων τῶν ἐν δικαιοσύνῃ (3:5)

---

39. Johnson, *Paul's Delegates*, 248.

The above list confirms the vital role of works in this letter. The repetition of the word reintroduces it in this section as a reminder of what works cannot do, namely render anyone righteous. Furthermore, while works cannot justify, believers will manifest good works and are shown to be genuine believers by their works. Works also serve as evidence that some are not part of God's family and are "worthless for any good work." Believers ought to be zealous for good works. Thus, the nature of an individual's works will reveal the existence or nonexistence of the knowledge of God. In this manner, the author is rhetorically strategic in his reintroduction of this key word.

Verse 5 also contains the much discussed phrase, διὰ λουτροῦ παλιγγενεσίας καὶ ἀνακαινώσεως, which emphasizes the newness of those who have encountered divine grace. Rhetorically, it functions to further the notion that those who have been renewed in this way are no longer what they used to be, since they have been regenerated and renewed. Thus, the good conduct espoused in 3:1–2 ought to be manifested by those who have been regenerated and renewed. By negative implication therefore, the absence of such conduct would testify to the fact that such individuals never experienced renewal and regeneration.

The certainty and completeness of the transformation is guaranteed by the Trinitarian references within the sentence. Failure to manifest godly conduct would amount to a denial of the salvific intervention of God the Father, Jesus Christ, and the Holy Spirit.

Verse 7 presents another instance of paronomasia in the participle δικαιωθέντες. Its rhetorical functions include highlighting again the contrast that is so endemic to this sentence (vv. 3–7). Other functions relate to intersectional cohesion since cognates of this word occur in 1:8 (δίκαιον), 2:12 (δικαίως), and 3:5 (δικαιοσύνη). Righteousness is a quality inherent to believers. Elder overseers must manifest it (1:8) as a requirement to serve in the church. Believers must live righteously, as they are instructed by grace (2:12). Righteousness manifests after salvation and cannot be attained by human efforts (3:5). Thus, the only time this positive quality is presented negatively is when it is viewed as attainable by works of righteousness. In every other instance, the word is presented as a positive Christian trait. In 3:7, the answer or explanation is given as to how a believer comes to manifest this quality: they are *made* righteous by divine grace. Likewise, in 2:11, it is grace that instructs believers to live "godly" (δικαίως) in this present age. The paronomasia serves to highlight the endemic nature of righteousness in the life of believers. Rhetorically, this has the effect of making genuine sainthood inseparable from the quality of righteousness. Thus, where this quality is absent it can reasonably be inferred that no salvation has occurred. The Cretans were not saved by righteous works they had done (οὐκ ἐξ ἔργων τῶν ἐν δικαιοσύνῃ); instead they were made righteous (δικαιωθέντες). In other words, they are passive in the act of acquiring the status of righteousness. The passive participle constitutes an emphatic denial of human boasting, contrasting directly with the sentiment expressed in the first part of v. 5. The use of inclusive language employed both in verbal and pronoun forms functions, among other things, to restrain any credit from accruing to human beings. Paul is implicitly affirming that even his Jewish heritage was of no value in his salvation or in acquiring this righteousness. Titus also has nothing to boast of apart from divine grace. By implication therefore, the Cretans are only saved by the gracious condescension of God who manifested ἔλεος.

Inclusive language also functions to foster a sense of community and identification. Paul, by indicating his own unworthiness to be saved, as well as that of Titus, facilitates thereby a full identification with the Cretans. The presentation of a Jew as a corecipient of divine grace must communicate powerfully against any temptations toward proud superiority. The rhetorical impact of this line of communication harnesses a sense of community and unity, while discouraging any latent allegiance to teachings and teachers that encourage the opposite.

In verse 7, we find the word χάρις, which is repeated from 2:11. The rhetorical objective of this repetition is to demonstrate the relationship between grace and righteousness. Here, it also concludes a conglomeration of related terms or synonyms used in this sentence to distinguish the divine action vis-à-vis the human action. From 3:4–7, the following terms are employed to describe God's behavior:

1. ἡ χρηστότης καὶ ἡ φιλανθρωπία (v. 4)
2. ἔλεος (v. 5)
3. χάριτι (v. 7)

This conglomeration is emphatic, highlighting the supremacy and totality of the divine action. In each of the above instances, the accompanying pronoun or modifier reiterates that with reference to the salvation of people, including the Cretans, God alone is the author thereof: *God's* kindness and love for mankind (τοῦ . . . θεοῦ), *God's* mercy (αὐτοῦ ἔλεος), and *God's* grace (ἐκείνου χάριτι). This triple emphasis stands in stark contrast to human effort with its emphatic first-person plural pronoun following after the verb: οὐκ ἐξ ἔργων τῶν ἐν διακαιοσύνῃ ἃ ἐποιήσαμεν ἡμεῖς.

The next two words in verse 7 are examples of kinship and inclusive language respectively. The noun κληρονόμος evokes images of family and privilege. Together with the verb γίνομαι, it serves as a very powerful confirmation of the transformation shared by all the believers without discrimination or exception. It is reminiscent of the earlier paternal reference to God as "our Father" (1:4) and parent-sibling images in which Paul calls Titus his "true child" (1:4). The verb γενηθῶμεν, being in the passive voice, reaffirms the consistent emphasis throughout this sentence on the passivity of humanity and the radical activity of God. The prepositional phrase, κατ' ἐλπίδα ζωῆς αἰωνίου, introduces a shift in the temporal emphasis of this sentence. Hope points to that which is still to come or to be expected, thus it points to some future event. More importantly though, this phrase repeats the reference in 1:2 where the apostle ties present godliness to the future hope (ἐπ' ἐλπίδι ζωῆς αἰωνίου). The repetition has the rhetorical effect of bolstering the coherency of the discourse, particularly as it also relates to 2:13 and the μακαραίαν. The three references to hope (ἐλπίς) impact on the temporal momentum of the discourse by introducing a future dimension to it. This future perspective serves an important rhetorical function. Positively, those who embrace sound doctrine and obey it can anticipate eternal life with its implicit rewards. Negatively, those who reject sound doctrine or who embrace false teaching are "warned" by the notion of a future reckoning. In other words, the teaching about the future serves to ground or anchor adherence to sound doctrine in the present while also warning those who risk ignoring sound doctrine. The obedient ones will have something good to look forward to, while those who are reckless in this life will, by implication, also have something to look forward to, but less pleasant.

The overall rhetorical effect of this future perspective is to communicate the truth that present godliness has future implications, while present ungodliness will also have future implications. This is an ingenious way to motivate the believers to embrace sound doctrine that results in godliness (1:1–2). Furthermore, the certainty of this hope is stressed by the triple repetition thereof throughout this letter. Additionally, in each of the theological sections, 1:1–4, and in 2:11–14 and 3:4–7, there is a transition in time frame—past, present, and future. Each relates how God has acted and how God's purposes were established. In this manner, the readers and hearers are given a "track record" or profile of God's actions. Logically, therefore, it can be deduced that if God has acted in the past and that action came to fruition, then the future (ἐλπίς) is certain.

CONCLUSION

The dominant rhetorical objective of verses 4–7, a single sentence in the original, is *to enforce compliance to sound doctrine by appealing to the divine example* through the reminder of God's salvific intervention. This section in particular has also not escaped the pervasiveness of the authenticity debate, which contributed to a mellow appreciation for the actual content of the sentence and the intent of the author. The approach to this sentence has centered upon three central issues: (a) the delineation of the passage and the degree to which this passage is considered representative of authentic Pauline work; (b) the interpretation of the word λουτρόν. In this regard, the evidence shows that continuity or discontinuity with Pauline theology impacts upon the interpretation of this word; (c) the nature of the passage, specifically whether it is a hymn or creed. Apart from these differences in opinion, there is widespread consensus surrounding the content of the sentence, particularly its soteriological nature. Scholars also recognize the unique Trinitarian emphases of the passage as well as its essential doctrinal character. While the text hints at baptism and salvation, it has been demonstrated that these are not the primary foci of the passage, and to insist that they are so does not advance our appreciation for the unique contribution of this letter.

The key aspect to appreciating this sentence is to interpret it in the order in which it appears. Such an approach reveals the intricate and powerful rhetorical argument that characterizes this sentence. Paul's overall rhetorical strategy is to hold before his audience the example of no one less than God. The behavior that they ought to conform to was demonstrated in their salvation by God. The divine attitude is set up as the standard by which to evaluate their own willingness or reluctance to comply with and manifest sound doctrine. It is suggested that this is the only objective the apostle sets out to achieve in this sentence. To this task, he draws from an arsenal of rhetorical techniques that were already used earlier on in the letter, with one exception, that of anthropopathism. He uses the latter to personalize God and to present God as an example not only to the saints but also to the disobedient, whose actions are showed to be glaringly inconsistent compared to that of the divine.

Minor rhetorical techniques utilized in this section include syndeton, implicit contrast, repetition, and paronomasia. It was demonstrated how strategic the repetition of ἔργον is in this section. Paronomasia of several words occurred, the most prominent being δικαιωθέντες. Other features include highly theological and inclusive language, like χρηστότης, φιλανθρωπία, ἔλεος, and χάρις. The language of inheritance calls to mind kinship, community, and inclusiveness. The orientation toward the future is reintroduced in this section through the expression κατ' ἐλπίδα ζωῆς αἰωνίου. This orientation functions rhetorically to, on the one hand, hold before the obedient the implicit promise of reward, while on the other hand, hint at negative consequences or punishment in the future to those who disobey now. The certainty of this hope is communicated by the triple repetition of the word *hope* throughout the letter, as well as by the recollection of God's consistency in the past. In this manner, the author uses the temporal momentum within this section as a guarantee of the future hope.

The sentence in itself functions as a rhetorical instrument. As was shown above, this sentence is one of three that are strategically located throughout this discourse. They are unique in character, revealing high concentrations of theological truths, probably known to the recipients. In the present example, scholars agree that the sentence constitutes preexistent traditional material or shared knowledge, known to the recipients. The fact that the recipients probably knew this material significantly adds to their persuasive value.

11

Titus 3:8–11

Reinforcing the Differences between Sound and Illegitimate Doctrine in Order to Encourage Compliance to the Former and Rejection of the Latter

IN THIS SECTION, 3:8–11, the author's dominant rhetorical objective is to make a final appeal for compliance to sound doctrine by *reinforcing the differences between sound and illegitimate doctrine*. He sets out to achieve this objective by encouraging the adoption of the one and the rejection of the other; in this case, it is false doctrine that must be rejected. As he nears the conclusion of his letter, he wants to help his audience maintain the mutual exclusivity of the opposing doctrines. Negatively, he wants to provide the congregation with some final reasons why they should forsake or not be lured to embrace false doctrine. This strategy is a repetition of that employed in 2:1–10. To accomplish this objective, Paul again contrasts sound doctrine with false doctrine, unleashing an assortment of rhetorical techniques to this end. In fact, this small section is unusually inundated with a variety of these techniques.

One scholar argues that this section contains the final contrast between sound doctrine and false doctrine, entitling this section as follows, "True and False Instruction."[1] Scholars are, however, divided on the exact demarcation of the section. There are those that argue it begins with the second part of verse 8 and indicate it as 8b–11.[2] Mounce views

1. Quinn, *Letter to Titus*, 233, 244.
2. Ibid., 233; Collins, *Timothy and Titus*, 366.

it as comprising 3:1–11.³ Knight, interestingly, includes it as part of 3:3–8, while Guthrie and Simpson argue that verse 8 commences a new section.⁴ There is, however, an alternative delineation.

The demarcation accepted in this analysis is based on the following arguments: Verse 8 should be viewed as separate from 4–7, because of a difference in genre. Verses 4–7 constitute some form of earlier tradition; that is, it could be a hymn or creed. Verse 8a is an observation about the preceding sentence and therefore not part of it. A final consideration, for the view that verse 8 begins a new section, relates to its function within the discourse. In this regard, consideration must be paid to the rhetorical intention behind this section.

The function of the sentence πιστός ὁ λόγος is multifaceted. It is one of three short sentences used in this section, with the others being ταῦτα ἐστιν καλὰ καὶ ὠφέλιμα τοῖς ἀωθρώποις (v. 8) and εἰσὶν γὰρ ἀνωφελεῖς καὶ μάταιοι (v. 9). Its brevity makes it conspicuous and highlights the claim that it makes about the previous section (vv. 4–7), which is one sentence. This, in itself, supports the decision for the division between the sections. The use of short sentences is one of several rhetorical techniques exploited in this section for emphatic purposes. At a basic level, the sentence serves to connect verses 8–11 with the preceding section, facilitating a degree of fluidity in this part of the apostle's argument. Later, it will be evident how it functions as an antithetic hedge with the description in verse 9 of the false teaching as ἀνωφελεῖς καὶ μάταιοι. Its immediate function, therefore, is transitional, indicating the transition from one genre form to another, i.e., from verses 4–7 to 8–11. At a rhetorical level, this statement functions as an apostolic affirmation of the preceding section. The apostle underscores the traditional material as πιστός ὁ λόγος. This is an important insight, if we want to appreciate the rest of his argument. The dominant rhetorical intent behind verses 8–11 is to contrast legitimate and illegitimate teaching in order to reinforce compliance to the former. Πιστός ὁ λόγος therefore should be interpreted to mean: "Everything said thus far constitute legitimate teaching. I affirm this to be so, in my capacity as δοῦλος θεοῦ, ἀπόστολος δὲ Ἰησοῦ Χριστοῦ" (1:1). Put in more colloquial terms, the apostle is saying something like this: "This is the real thing." The first-person singular, βούλομαι, suggests the

---

3. Mounce, *Pastoral Epistles*, 434, 455.

4. Guthrie, *Pastoral Epistles*, 207; Simpson, *Greek Text*, 116; Knight, *Pastoral Epistles*, 350.

reasonableness of such an interpretation of the text. This sentence therefore introduces the first reason why sound teaching is to be embraced as well as why it is superior to false teaching. This is an argument based on apostolic authorization. Sound doctrine must be heeded because unlike false teaching, it is apostolically authorized. In the rest of the sentence, the apostle is going to give two more reasons why Cretan believers must comply with sound doctrine and reject false doctrine.

The second half of verse 8 builds upon the first part. Since these teachings are legitimate, the apostle proceeds to express his desire (βούλομαι) that Titus should insist or speak confidently (διαβεβαιοόμαι) about them. The strong διαβεβαιοόμαι leads Mounce to interpret τούτων as referring to all of chapter 3.[5] Knight agrees, arguing that it refers to 3:1–7, while Hendriksen limits it to verses 4–7.[6] Contextually, it is more tenable to argue that the pronoun refers to everything that has gone before till now and not only to 3:4–7. The ensuing purpose clause includes the key expression καλῶν ἔργων, which could tenably be interpreted to include the virtues commended in 3:1–2.

Earlier, in 2:1, Titus was exhorted to "speak" (λάλεω). In contradistinction, in 1:11, the false teachers must be silenced (ἐπιστομίζω). Thus, sound doctrine can be spoken about confidently. This command, like the earlier ones, is an instance of apostolic affirmation or authorization of the ministry of Titus.

The purpose clause ἵνα . . . θεῷ has a very interesting structure. The preposition ἵνα is followed by the verb φροντίζωσιν. These two are separated from the infinitive προΐστασθαι and the subject, οἱ πεπιστευκότες, by the key expression καλῶν ἔργων. It is only at the end that the subject, οἱ πεπιστευκότες, is revealed. This structure emphasizes a concern or eagerness for good works. Thus, Titus must insist or speak confidently so that a concern or eagerness for sound doctrine will result or be manifested. The emphasis in the second part of this sentence is that only those who believed and continue to believe in God are able to be occupied in good works. The participle, πεπιστευκότες, is in the perfect tense and expresses the idea of a completed action perpetuated in the present. The faith allegiance of those who are careful to perform good deeds is directed toward God, θεῷ. The juxtaposition of the subject and indirect object stresses the inseparability of faith in God and good works. Put differently, those who

---

5. Mounce, *Pastoral Epistles*, 452.
6. Knight, *Pastoral Epistles*, 350; Hendriksen, *Timothy and Titus*, 394.

believe in God will be those who perform καλὰ ἔργα. This is in direct opposition to the false teachers who profess to know God but deny God by their deeds: θεὸν ὁμολογοῦσιν εἰδέναι, τοῖς δὲ ἔργοις ἀρνοῦνται (1:16). In this way, the chasm between the two groups is accentuated and the disparities are made all the more obvious. This constitutes an argument based upon the *irreconcilability of conduct*. Thus, the second reason why sound teaching is different relates to the ensuing good works, which, in turn, confirm those who perform them as the ones who actually have come to faith in God. The substantive use of the participle supports the notion of identity. Here, the apostle uses the rhetorical technique of *honorific referencing* to encourage compliance to sound doctrine. Thus, through behavior compliant to sound doctrine, the audience will demonstrate their faith or the absence of faith in God. The Cretans must decide whether they deserve the honor of being referred to as οἱ πεπιστευκότες θεῷ or not; only their conduct will show this.

Another distinction from false doctrine is the beneficial impact of sound doctrine and resulting deeds upon the rest of society. The last part of verse 8 contains the final reason for compliance to sound doctrine, namely its positive impact upon the rest of humanity. These things, i.e., all the teaching contained in chapter 3, are καλὰ καὶ ὠφέλιμα τοῖς ἀωθρώποις. The use of syndeton emphasizes the double significance of the sound doctrine. Several words are repeated in this section and each instance is emphatic. The word καλόν repeats within a single sentence an earlier occurrence, namely καλῶν ἔργων. The hearers would hear this double reiteration of "good," which in turn, connects this section with all the earlier occurrences of this word. The word ἄνθρωπος recalls several occurrences of this noun, some of which are positive while one or two are negative. In 3:2, the believers are called to exhibit kindness πρὸς πάντας ἀνθρώπους. Grace appeared πᾶσιν ἀνθρώποις (2:11). Both of these could be classified as positive uses of this word. The first negative occurrence is in 1:14 with reference to the false teachers who adhere to the commandments of men (ἐντολαῖς ἀνθρώπων). Within the immediate context of 3:8–11, the word appears again, but in a negative context, with reference to the opposition who are αἱρετικὸν ἄνθρωπον. In 3:8, the intention is surely to accentuate the positive benefits of sound doctrine to the greater humanity, similar to 2:11 with regard to grace. Rhetorically, the intention to contrast the positive effect of sound doctrine with the negative effect of false doctrine cannot be clearer. False teaching was "upsetting whole households" (ὅλους οἴκους ἀνατρέπουσιν) (1:11); this cannot be maintained about sound doctrine. The repetition of ἄνθρωπος serves the additional purpose of facilitating coherence throughout the letter or facilitating intersectional coherence.

Thus, in verse 8, the apostle has successfully highlighted the distinctiveness of sound doctrine. Sound doctrine is commended by the apostolic affirmation in the sentence πιστὸς ὁ λόγος. The results of sound doctrine can be seen by the good works that those who believe in God will be careful to perform. Finally, the good works will benefit the community at large. Through repetition of key words, the apostle facilitates implicit contrasts with the opposition from earlier sections of the letter. The highly positive presentation of sound doctrine is the main rhetorical intent of verse 8. In the next section, the contrast between sound and false doctrine is perpetuated, but this time through an intensely negative portrayal of the opposition.

The primary rhetorical intent in 3:9–11 is the perpetuation of the contrast between sound and false doctrine. This section is replete with rhetorical techniques employed to achieve the rhetorical objective, namely to encourage the audience to reject false doctrine. However, commentators reveal an etymological preoccupation with the vocabulary in this and other sentences, although they sometimes cite some helpful extrabiblical occurrences of the words.[7] However, as a result of this focus, they do not pay much attention to the other stylistic features present in this section. Mounce and Knight, for example, categorize μωρὰς δὲ ζητήσεις καὶ γενεαλογίας καὶ ἔρεις καὶ μάχας νομικὰς as merely a list of "errors to avoid."[8] There are those who draw attention to the polysyndeton in this sentence but unfortunately fail to explain its function in the sentence.[9] This will now be addressed.

Verse 9 opens with the adversative δέ followed by four references to the false teaching, each separated by the conjunction καί. The function of the adversative conjunction, according to Mounce, is to "establish . . . contrast."[10] He unfortunately limits the contrast exclusively to this chapter, whereas it is best understood to perpetuate the contrast that runs consistently throughout the letter. In all fairness to him, there

---

7. Simpson, *Greek Text*, 117–18; Quinn, *Letter to Titus*, 244–48.
8. Mounce, *Pastoral Epistles*, 453; Knight, *Pastoral Epistles*, 353–54.
9. Collins, *Timothy and Titus*, 368; Quinn, *Letter to Titus*, 245.
10. Mounce, *Pastoral Epistles*, 453.

is definitely a contrast in the immediate context, but it transcends the context, as the analysis of this section will show, and as the repetition of key vocabulary in verse 8 has demonstrated. This verse sports the rhetorical technique called polysyndeton. The four descriptions of the false teaching are separated by three conjunctions: μωρὰς (δὲ) ζητήσεις καὶ γενεαλογίας καὶ ἔρεις καὶ μάχας νομικάς. The polysyndeton emphasizes the false teaching. The rhetorical objective behind it is the vilification of the false teaching. The terms are largely negative, almost mocking. The false teaching must not be confronted, instead Titus must "steer clear" from or "avoid" (περιΐστημι) it. The imperative indicates that the problem is not endemic to the congregation. It is not something to get rid of; rather, it is to be avoided. Rhetorically, and as far as Paul is concerned, false doctrine is invalid, unnecessary, not worthy of Titus's consideration or time. It is, by implication, an utter waste of time. This is therefore, a clear instance of vilification. Here, it is the false teaching itself that is vilified rather than its promoters (cf. 1:10–16). The polysyndeton accentuates the worthlessness and futility of the false teaching. The reason given in the second half of this verse reinforces the uselessness of the teaching: εἰσὶν γὰρ ἀνωφελεῖς καὶ μάταιοι. The polarity between sound and false doctrine is accentuated by opposing terms used to describe both. In 8:1, sound doctrine was affirmed to be πιστὸς ὁ λόγος. Verse 9 concludes with a judgment on false doctrine being ἀνωφελεῖς καὶ μάταιοι. The latter expression constitutes an apostolic denunciation of the false teaching. This denunciation could be seen as an additional evidence for the distinctiveness of sound doctrine. Rhetorically, therefore, anyone who embraces false teaching would be affirming that which the apostle has judged to be "worthless and unprofitable." It would place such a person in the very awkward position of going against the judgment of a "servant of God and an apostle of Jesus Christ" (1:1).

The positive/negative disparity is reiterated through the employment of several smaller rhetorical techniques of which some have already been pointed out earlier. Verses 8–11 contain several antonyms: sound doctrine was considered profitable (ὠφέλιμα) (v. 8). False teaching on the other hand is condemned as unprofitable, (ἀνωφελεῖς) (v. 9). Paul brands false teachings as "quarrels," (μάχας) (3:9) but wants believers to be "peaceable," (ἀμάχους) (3:2). Another contrast is drawn through the choice of words used to describe people in this section. In verse 8, believers are spoken of honorably as οἱ πεπιστευκότες θεῷ, while the false teacher is labeled a αἱρετικὸν ἄνθρωπον (v. 10). When compared to earlier sections, a progression can be observed with regard to the increasing discrimination between the opposing parties in the letter. In 1:9, the elder overseer must oppose τοὺς ἀντιλέγοντας. Here, the opponents are represented by the reference to the singular αἱρετικὸν ἄνθρωπον. This is an instance of the rhetorical technique of synecdoche. Furthermore, there is progression: from confrontation or ἐλέγχειν (1:9), to censuring, ἐπιστομίζειν (1:11), to avoidance of the doctrine (3:9), and, finally, shunning of the person, παραιτέομαι (3:10). There can clearly be no compromise between those who teach and adhere to sound doctrine and those who teach and embrace false doctrine. The chasm only becomes wider. The paronomasia by the use of the two words, "empty talkers" (ματαιολόγοι) (1:10) and "empty" (μάταιοι) (3:9) does not paint a very complimentary picture of the false teachers or their doctrine.

Through syndeton, ἀνωφελεῖς καὶ μάταιοι, the groundless futility of false teaching is emphasized while at the same time its distinctiveness from sound doctrine is accentuated. Sound teaching is also emphasized through syndeton positively as καλὰ καὶ ὠφέλιμα. The syndeton of verse 10, μίαν καὶ δευτέραν, emphasizes the specificity of the manner in which erroneous teachings must be treated. No tolerance must be entertained, just two warnings followed by shunning or rejection. The apostle seems to show great awareness of the insidiousness of false teaching to the church. This alone could justify the severe treatment advocated so emphatically here.

Verse 11 drives home the proverbial final nail in the coffin through emphatic clustering of verbs that describe the false teacher: ἐξέστραπται (ὁ τοιοῦτος) καὶ ἁμαρτάνει ὢν αὐτοκατάκριτος. This is akin to the vilification section of chapter 1. In the present section, the apostle has vilified not only their teaching but also the person of the teachers and accentuates it through emphatic clustering. The description portrays a gradual downward progression from perversion, to sinning, to the final state of self-condemnation.

CONCLUSION

The dominant rhetorical objective of this section is *to reinforce the differences between sound and illegitimate doctrine in order to encourage compliance to the former and rejection of the latter*. The argument is structured by way of contrast to highlight the virtues of one over the other. Thus, verse 8 contains reasons for the adoption of sound doctrine while verses 9–11 provide reasons for the rejection of false teaching. This task is accomplished through the employment of an array of rhetorical techniques. Rhetorical techniques employed include syndeton, polysyndeton, antonyms, repetition, synecdoche, paronomasia, and emphatic clustering. The opening sentence is one of three very short sentences in this section and is used to emphasize the resultant contrast between sound and false doctrine.

The apostle highlights three characteristics of sound doctrine, namely the apostolic commendation thereof, its association with those who have come to faith in God, and finally its beneficial impact upon the rest of society.

The author manages to animate the remembrance of the opposition, mentioned in earlier parts of the letter, by applying, in this section, the following positive words to believers, namely καλόν, ἔργον, καλά, and ἄνθρωπος. Their employment results in a condition I call *implicit contrasting* of the polarized groups in the letter. This choice of vocabulary and its application to believers contribute to a highly positive presentation of sound doctrine.

In verses 9–11, the negative aspects of the false doctrine are highlighted. This section has much in common with chapter 1, repeating similar tones and sentiments. The apostle basically vilifies the false teaching in 3:9, contrasting its negative impact with that of sound doctrine through the use of another short sentence, εἰσὶν γὰρ ἀνωφελεῖς καὶ μάταιοι. In verses 10–11, he vilifies the person of the false teacher and uses name calling or labeling, as he did in 1:10. The effect of all this criticism and commendation is that the chasm between sound and false doctrine is maintained, if not reinforced. It removes any possibility for compromise between the two parties. Clearly, the intent of the author, toward the end of his letter, is to hold before his audience two pictures, one of false doctrine and another of sound doctrine, showing them why they should comply with the latter and reject the former. They cannot but choose sound doctrine and reject the other, because this puts them in community with the apostle who authorizes sound doctrine. Furthermore, it confirms their identity as those who believe in God when they order their conduct in line with sound doctrine.

12

Titus 3:12–15

Adapting the Conclusion to Reinforce the Notion of Legitimate Ministry

SCHOLARS REGARD THE CLOSING section as a "standard" Pauline text.[1] While all the standard elements of a Pauline conclusion are present, the vocabulary and the rich network of cognate linguistic concepts suggest that Paul is adapting his normal conclusion for a more important purpose, namely to round off his overall argument for compliance to sound doctrine, especially reemphasizing the notion of legitimate ministry. This is the ideal opportunity, seeing that he has just in the previous section (vv. 9–11) addressed illegitimate ministry and dictated measures to deal with the false teacher(s). The conclusion leaves the recipients in no doubt as to what constitutes legitimate ministry.

This is a very tight unit, which is carefully, almost abruptly, demarcated from the preceding section through repetition and paronomasia. There is, however, a clear transition in terms from the perspective of the content of this section; it deals with practical and personal arrangements. Based on this, scholars like Quinn argue that the unit should be read exclusively with the opening verses as a "compositional envelope," instead of with the preceding sections.[2] Paronomasia and repetition do seem to suggest some correspondence with the opening sections. Quinn points out several examples: λείπῃ (3:13) and ἀπέλιπον . . . τά λείποντα

---

1. See Demarest, *Timothy, Titus*, 331; Knight, *Pastoral Epistles*, 356; Mounce, *Pastoral Epistles*, 456, 459.

2. Quinn, *Letter to Titus*, 260.

(1:5), ἐν πίστει (3:15) and κατὰ κοινὴν πίστιν (1:4), χάρις (3:15b) and the same in 1:4, 5. The unity of this section is underscored by the repetition of the following words in rapid succession to each other: πέμψω (v. 12) and its cognate πρόπεμψον (v. 13), σπούδασον (v. 12) and the adverb σπουδαίως (v. 13). Quinn adds οἱ ἡμέτεροι (v. 14) and ἡμᾶς (v. 15).[3] Verse 15 discloses an interesting repetition of the verb ἀσπάζομαι and the adjective πᾶς within a single verse. The repetition serves to emphasize the important function of the greetings, in particular its enhancement of the sense of community. It furthermore affirms the legitimacy of the believers at Crete. The greeting from those who are geographically separated from them serves as affirmation of unity; it reinforces that they belong. The same holds true for Titus, for whom this greeting is a reminder that he is not serving in isolation but as part of a community.

The emphasis of this final section recalls and rejoins the opening verses of this letter but not initially in as strong a manner as Quinn insists upon. With due respect to Quinn, there remain sufficient reasons to argue for a close connection between this section and the preceding units. The word πίστος and its cognates appear nine times in this letter, in five different forms scattered throughout each chapter (1:1, 4, 6, 9, 13; 2:2, 10; 3:8, 15). The word χάρις also appears elsewhere in 1:11, 2:11, and 3:7. The repetition of these words facilitates coherence within the letter rather than just establishing a link between two isolated units. Furthermore, overemphasizing the abruptness of the unit suggests that there is very little relationship with the previous section. On the contrary, there is a very deliberate link between the two sections when considered from a rhetorical perspective. The abruptness facilitates a mental break from a chilling presentation of the negative consequences for rejecting sound doctrine (v. 11). It also introduces a positive picture of legitimate ministry and ministers. It is here where the link with the opening verses is strongest, and credit must go to Quinn for his observations in this regard.

The dominant rhetorical emphasis of this section is upon the notion of legitimate ministry. No overt contrasts are presented, and no new propositions are introduced. In fact, this part of the letter points back to concepts introduced in the opening of the letter.

In verse 12, Paul introduces measures to ensure the perpetuation of legitimate ministry in Crete. He had just advised them to reject the false teacher (3:10). Now he is about to introduce legitimate ministry. The

3. Quinn, *Letter to Titus*, 260.

duration of Titus's ministry is limited, and a replacement will be sent in the future. Collins considers the introduction of the four characters, Artemis, Tychicus, Zenas and Apollos an outstanding characteristic of this conclusion.[4] The fact that Paul plans to send a replacement rather than transfer responsibility for ministry to the elder overseers is suggestive of the relative young age of the church in Crete. Hendriksen observes in his regard that "churches cannot be made 'indigenous' overnight. As long as leadership from the outside is necessary, it must be provided."[5] The kind of legitimate ministry envisaged is similar to that introduced in opening portions of the letter. Whereas the ministry of Paul has divine sanction, subsequent ministry must enjoy apostolic sanction in order to prove legitimate. Such ministry must harmonize with that of the apostle, with regard to doctrine.

The provision of ministerial successors furthermore functions to present a positive picture of Paul. He is portrayed as one deeply concerned about the church and expresses such care through the careful appointment of sound leaders. This is what led him to leave Titus there in the first place (1:5), and now he remains unwavering in his commitment to them. Furthermore, Paul wants to ensure that the church continues to receive sound doctrine which, in turn, requires the presence of sound teachers, hence Artemis or Tychicus. The use of the first-person singular verb πέμψω confirms that it is Paul who will be sending one of them.

Additionally, by expressing the desire for Titus's presence, the apostle says much about the latter's reputation with the apostle. The ministry of Titus has constantly been affirmed throughout this letter. Presently, this request that Titus join the apostle (σπούδασον ἐλθεῖν πρός με εἰς Νικόπολιν) functions in a similar manner. It affirms the present ministry of Titus while still in Crete. In the eyes of the congregation, Titus is presented as one whose company the apostle seeks. Thus, if the apostle Paul appreciates Titus, how much more should the Cretans? How privileged they are to have him minister among them. If the Cretans were harboring any secret wish for a visit from the apostle, such desire is disappointed by the present arrangements as well as by the information that he will be spending the winter in Nicopolis (ἐκεῖ γὰρ κέκρικα παραχειμάσαι).

What is very clear is that the perpetuation of legitimate ministry does not require the physical presence of an apostle, only the presence of

---

4. Collins, *Timothy and Titus*, 370.
5. Hendriksen, *Timothy and Titus*, 398.

those committed to the teaching, which would eventually include elder overseers from their own ranks (1:9).

The list of names in this section also introduces at least four other men who uphold legitimate teaching and who are committed to that which the apostle is committed to, namely the integrity and perpetuation of sound doctrine among the believers. These are men who care about them, unlike the false teachers who teach from selfish and exploitative motives (1:11).

The list of names functions rhetorically to highlight again the notion of legitimate ministry. Proper names are only mentioned here and in the introductory parts of the letter. In this manner, the closing section functions beautifully to round off the letter. Interestingly, though, the false teachers remain nameless.

Verse 14 is rhetorically significant since the apostle includes a final exhortation for good works. This reiterates the lesson of the entire letter: that sound doctrine results in a healthy ethic. The opportunity that is presented to them is to provide practical help to those committed to legitimate teaching, Zenas and Apollos. The verb, μανθάνω, is one of four synonyms used in the letter to refer to teaching and learning: διδασκαλία (1:9, 11; 2:1, 7, 10), καλοδιδασκάλος (2:3), σωφρονίζω (2:4), and παιδεύω (2:12). The word implies the existence of an attitude that responds to teaching and results in the performance of good deeds. Those who respond positively to teaching are described as "our ones/people" (οἱ ἡμέτεροι). This is an instance of *honorific referencing* or classification and is rhetorically significant because anyone who refuses to practice good deeds demonstrates by that refusal that he or she does not belong to the people of Paul and his delegates. The expression καλῶν ἔργων προΐστασθαι repeats an earlier occurrence (3:8). In the latter appearance, those who performed good works were described as οἱ πεπιστευκότες θεῷ. Here, they are *honorifically referenced or classified* as οἱ ἡμέτεροι. Thus, legitimate teaching results in sound doctrine, which results in good deeds by those who submit to it, demonstrating by it that they believe in God or are in community with the apostles, the delegates, and the rest of the churches. The honorific reference serves to reinforce their identity and to distinguish them from the false teachers and their followers. More importantly, it serves as a final reinforcement of the inseparability of sound doctrine and good deeds. The purpose clause, ἵνα μὴ ὦσιν ἄκαρποι, uses an agricultural metaphor, and restates in the negative (ἄκαρποι) the necessity to bear fruit. The believer's good works are his or her fruit. A fruit tree benefits others when it does what a fruit tree does, namely bear fruit.

The closing greetings in verse 15 reinforces a sense of community and functions as an encouragement to the recipients. Interestingly, Titus receives a separate greeting from the rest of the congregation. Perhaps this serves again to reiterate the prominence of Titus to other believers, οἱ (μετ' ἐμοῦ) πάντες and hence to affirm him in the eyes of the Cretan believers, in line with the endearing manner in which he is referred to in the salutation (1:4). The closing greeting to the Cretans involves another instance of *honorific referencing or classification*. They are called τοὺς φιλοῦντας ἡμᾶς ἐν πίστει. This expression serves a vicarious function, firstly as a term of endearment—an affectionate reference to the congregations in Crete. The verb φιλέω is an instance of paronomasia at this late stage in the letter. The cognate words were used in the context of family relationships in 2:4 and with reference to elder overseers in 1:8. Wives must love their husbands and children, φιλάνδρος and φιλοτέκνος respectively, while local leaders must demonstrate hospitality (literally: love strangers) and be lovers of good, φιλόξενον and φιλάγαθον respectively. Seen from this perspective the verb, φιλέω positively reinforces the idea of family love, community, and intimacy. It serves to draw Paul and the others with him relationally closer to the believers at Crete. The second and negative nuance relates to the limitation that is established through the expression ἐν πίστει. In other words, it excludes those who are not "in (the) faith." Paul's greeting is therefore limited to those who are in the faith and to no one else—only to those who are of the same family, who are οἱ ἡμέτεροι (v. 14). The Cretans are again forced to recognize that one can be "in (the) faith" or negatively "out of (the) faith." This kind of eradication of grey areas is consistent with Paul's argument throughout the letter. He remains uncompromising to the very end, although it must be added that the choice of vocabulary "softens" the reality of what he is saying in this concluding part of his letter.

This gentle tone culminates in the final sentence by taking the form of a blessing directed to all the believers: Ἡ χάρις μετὰ πάντων ὑμῶν. The rhetorical function of this blessing is to encourage them as recipients of divine favor.[6] The blessing represents the final appearance of the key word, χάρις, used first in the salutation and scattered throughout the

---

6. Tolmie, *Persuading the Galatians*, 223-24.

letter. The blessing concludes this letter in a positive tone and brings together the opening and conclusion of the letter.

CONCLUSION

The dominant rhetorical objective of this section is *to reinforce the notion of legitimate teaching*. This is accomplished through the use of a list of workers that are representative of sound doctrine. The legitimacy of their ministry stems from the apostolic mandate or affirmation thereof. Titus is also affirmed, on the basis of the value the apostle attaches to his company. The list of workers furthermore demonstrates the apostolic concern and care for the congregation. Through *honorific referencing*, the congregation is referred to in different ways such as "our people," those who are "in faith" and "those who love us." The legitimacy of the teaching will be evident by their readiness to perform good deeds to meet urgent needs. This is a point raised by way of reminder. There is also the regular use of repetition and paronomasia. The particular repetition of key words from the introductory portions of this letter adds to the feeling of an argument that has gone full circle. The final rhetorical technique is the concluding blessing, which functions as an encouragement to all the saints with the emphatic employment of the adjective πάς.

13

Conclusion

Layered Structural Coherence

PAUL DID NOT WRITE merely to transmit information. He wrote to *persuade*. The original hypothesis guiding the dissertation from which this book originates reads as follows: *A thorough text-centered rhetorical approach to the Letter of Titus (i.e., without relating it to the other two Pastoral Letters or approaching it in terms of the authenticity/inauthenticity debate) will yield new insights for its interpretation*. Since then, I've renamed the methodology from text-centered rhetorical analysis to *text-generated persuasion analysis*, a name that avoids the baggage associated with the word "rhetoric" or "rhetorical" and is a more accurate description of what actually occurs within a text, particularly a New Testament epistle. In a future publication, I hope to elaborate and systematize the methodology developed by my *Doktorvater*, D. F. Tolmie.

Analysis of the persuasive strategies or intent sheds fascinating light on the structure of the letter. Indeed, there is evidence of multiple or layered structural levels. But first, I will summarize something of the modest contribution here proposed.

The important question to be asked now is, did this study indeed yield new insights, as foreseen in the opening sections? To begin, it should be pointed out that this study is the only comprehensive analysis—as well as the only contemporary text-centered (text-generated), rhetorical (persuasion) analysis—of the Letter to Titus. Rhetorical interest in the Pastorals is generally rare, and in the case of Titus, it is virtually nonexistent. With regard to Titus, it has been suggested that this is attributable, firstly, to the relative novelty of the rhetorical critical approach and, secondly, to the brevity of the letter in comparison to the other two letters. Titus is often treated as a footnote within the greater discussion of the Timothean corpus, with the exception of the studies discussed earlier. Unfortunately, even these do not investigate *persuasion* in the letter; the investigation is exegetical rather than rhetorically oriented; it does not provide a *comprehensive* rhetorical treatment of the letter, whereas I focus specifically on the issue of persuasion more comprehensively, employing a totally different rhetorical approach. Of course, these claims are open for evaluation by other scholars.

Furthermore, it is hoped that the detailed analyses presented in the preceding chapters provide new insights into the details of the rhetorical or persuasive strategy both in terms of the way in which the dominant rhetorical strategy of a particular section could be described, as well as how the discussion of the detailed issues are related to this strategy. These will not be repeated here. Instead, the focus will now fall on the *overall rhetorical strategy* in the letter. This can be approached from different angles, namely by looking at (a) the *step-by-step development* of the overall argument, (b) the overall rhetorical (persuasive) strategy in terms of the *holistic chronological development* of the argument, and (c) the *contiguous development between the dominant (persuasive) objectives*.

Step-by-Step Development

1. Titus 1:1–4: Adapting the salutation to emphasize the divine basis of legitimate ministry
2. Titus 1:5–9: Outlining the criteria for legitimate local leadership
3. Titus 1:10–16: Discrediting the illegitimate teachers
4. Titus 2:1: Distinguishing Titus as a minister of sound doctrine on the basis of apostolic authorization
5. Titus 2:2–10: Persuading the Cretans that personal conduct compliant with sound doctrine is compulsory and should characterize all believers
6. Titus 2:11–15: Emphasizing the divine basis of obedience to sound doctrine
7. Titus 3:1–2: Persuading the Cretans of the compulsory treatment of all unbelievers in a manner consistent with sound doctrine

8. Titus 3:3: Evoking disgust with past sinful behavior in order to reinforce behavior in the present that complies with sound doctrine

9. Titus 3:4-7: Persuading the Cretans that displaying good works to those considered undeserving conforms to the divine example

10. Titus 3:8-11: Reinforcing the differences between sound and illegitimate doctrine in order to encourage compliance to the former and rejection of the latter

11. Titus 3:12-15: Adapting the conclusion to reemphasize the notion of legitimate ministry

The above outline evinces certain thematic repetitions or emphases. For example, the opening and closing units both emphasize legitimate teaching. Units 5 and 7 raise the issue of compliant behavior while units 1, 6, and 9 evince a distinctly theological character. The variation in the units raises the question of whether these apparent thematic commonalities are deliberate creations, part of the author's overall rhetorical strategy, or whether they are incidental, a random expression of unrelated ideas. More important is the question of whether any coherent pattern suggestive of an overall rhetorical strategy is discernible from these summaries. The answer: definitely!

The three theological sections (units 1, 6, and 9), each comprising one long sentence, are complimented by three sections that describe or relate to certain behavior. The complimentary sections include 1:5-16, 2:1-10, and 3:1-3, respectively. Within their respective contexts, the three theological sections are programmatic for identifying a step-by-step development of Paul's overall rhetorical strategy in the letter.

Holistic Chronological Development

Let us next consider the overall rhetorical objective. The apostle opens the letter giving a very clear indication of his mandate as a servant and an apostle (1:1), namely that he serves in this capacity κατὰ πίστιν ἐκλεκτῶν θεοῦ καὶ ἐπίγνωσιν ἀληθείας τῆς κατ' εὐσέβειαν. The objectives of his ministry relate to the divinely elect ones who are characterized by very particular behavior. This initial emphasis, therefore, is suggestive of the problem that the Cretans were being confronted with, namely the threat of compromising the high standard of living in the present life, namely godliness, κατ' εὐσέβειαν. Thus, in 1:16, the key characteristic of the agitators is their paradoxical profession of God and their denial of God by their deeds or works: ἃ θεὸν ὁμολογοῦσιν εἰδέναι, τοῖς δὲ ἔργοις ἀρνοῦνται. The objective of the apostle, therefore, relates to the *maintenance or restoration of the following balance: deeds that affirm and correspond to the testimony of faith in God*. Behavior, however, does not happen in a vacuum, but is influenced, if not determined by, doctrine. In the letter, we have two groups of teachers with opposing doctrines competing for the same audience. Paul, in 1:1, informs the audience that he is a minister "for the knowledge of the truth" (ἐπίγνωσιν ἀληθείας). The overall rhetorical objective is thus related to the notion of doctrinal quality. The congregation must be persuaded to embrace healthy doctrine, while rejecting unhealthy doctrine based upon the submission of convincing evidence. In the light of these considerations, I submit that the following four-stage overall rhetorical strategy underlies the letter.

First stage: 1:1–16: *Convince the audience of the transcendent character of the origin of legitimate teaching and of those who teach it.*

This stage in the overall rhetorical strategy underlies the first three units identified in the rhetorical analysis:

1. Titus 1:1–4: Adapting the salutation to emphasize the divine basis of legitimate ministry
2. Titus 1:5–9: Outlining the criteria for legitimate local leadership
3. Titus 1:10–16: Discrediting the illegitimate teachers

The first thing the apostle needs to do is to persuade the Cretans to distinguish between "doctrine" and "doctrine," as well as between "teachers" and "teachers." Legitimate teaching is "the truth" (1:1); it comes from God through designated office bearers who include apostles, delegates of the apostles, and lay leaders appointed by the apostolic delegate (1:1–9). The conduct of the lay leaders combined with a thorough commitment to the "faithful word" (1:9) is what sets them apart from the illegitimate teachers who are vilified and ultimately shown to have no relationship with God (1:16). In other words, the false teachers are shown to be illegitimate by their conduct as well as by the absence of divine legitimization of their persons. In this way, the transcendent character of legitimate teaching is emphasized and tries to counter an attitude that seems to reason that teaching is teaching and teachers are teachers. This transcendence relates to the origin of the teaching and the authorization of the teachers. A relationship is set up between legitimate teaching and the theological origin thereof. Thus, this section attempts to show that sound doctrine is legitimate. It is transcendent because its origin is divine. Those who are authorized to teach sound doctrine derive their authorization from its transcendent source, namely God. Conversely, teachings and teachers that are not divinely authorized or theologically justifiable are invalid and of no benefit to the church. Where that transcendent source or divine link between the teaching and the teachers is absent, both must be rejected.

Second stage: 2:1–15: *Convince the audience of the transcendent character of behavior accompanying legitimate teaching.*

This stage in the overall rhetorical objective underlies units 4–6 identified in the rhetorical analysis of the letter:

4. Titus 2:1: Distinguishing Titus as a minister of sound doctrine on the basis of apostolic authorization

5. Titus 2:2–10: Persuading the Cretans that personal conduct compliant with sound doctrine is compulsory and should characterize all believers

6. Titus 2:11–15: Emphasizing the divine basis of obedience to sound doctrine

This stage begins with the authorization of Titus's ministry in unit 4 (2:1), which really distinguishes it from what was said of the illegitimate teachers (1:10–16). Unit 5 (2:2–10) contains descriptions of behavior by various categories of believers that constitute manifestations of compliance to sound doctrine. The next unit (2:11–15) explains the specified conduct in theological terms. This has the effect of elevating the behavior to a divine level, which highlights the transcendent character of the behavior. At one level, the required behavior is what society in general would commend. However, the conduct of believers becomes a manifestation of a divine reality, namely the appearance of grace in the life of believers. If believers were asked to explain their conduct, they would respond something like this: "Our teacher is grace who teaches us to conduct ourselves in this manner. In other words, believers are not merely manifesting behavior that society deems good." The behavior of believers is thus motivated by a transcendent cause or motive, namely the appearance of grace and the complete transformation that they have experienced (2:11–15). They are behaving like God's people, living in anticipation of the appearance of Jesus Christ (2:12); they are a redeemed people, a cleansed people, zealous for good works (2:13). Thus, the believers are not simply practicing good manners; instead, their behavior is explicable by theological reasons. There is a theological basis to explain why believers conduct themselves the way they do. Thus, there is nothing "ordinary" about the way Christians ought to behave.

Third stage: 3:1–7: *Convince the audience of the transcendent character of their relationships with secular society.*

This stage in the rhetorical strategy underlies units 7–9 identified in the rhetorical analysis:

7. Titus 3:1–2: Persuading the Cretans of the compulsory treatment of all unbelievers in a manner consistent with sound doctrine

8. Titus 3:3: Evoking disgust with past sinful behavior in order to reinforce behavior in the present that complies with sound doctrine

9. Titus 3:4–7: Persuading the Cretans that displaying good works to those considered undeserving demonstrates conforms to the divine example

In unit 7 (3:1–2), the relationship of believers to their secular environment comes under the spotlight. It appears as if the false teaching encouraged a withdrawal from or even hostility toward secular society. Based upon the existence of prior knowledge, Paul argues that the Cretans already know how to conduct themselves toward secular authorities. In unit 8 (3:3), the apostle uses the rhetorical technique of *self-vilification* to inspire disgust. His intention is likely that he wants to persuade the Cretans to behave properly toward secular society. The transcendent motivation for their behavior is provided in unit 9 (3:4–7). God acted kindly toward the Cretans when they were least deserving of it. Their attitude toward secular society is, therefore, more than just decent citizenship; it follows the transcendent example of God.

Fourth stage: 3:8–15: *Convince the audience that only one of two positions is possible by reemphasizing that one either does or does not belong to the community.*

In units 10 and 11, the concluding stage in the rhetorical strategy follows:

10. Titus 3:8–11: Reinforcing the differences between sound and illegitimate doctrine in order to encourage compliance to the former and rejection of the latter

11. Titus 3:12–15: Adapting the conclusion to reemphasize the notion of legitimate ministry

In summary: The overall rhetorical objective relates to the use of theological motivations for the adoption of sound doctrine and the practice of sound behavior by the Cretans. Sound doctrine and corresponding behavior are inseparably connected to a theological basis, namely the manifestation of "God's word" (1:3), "God's grace" (2:11), and "God's kindness and love for mankind" (3:4). Thus, the doctrine is portrayed as transcendent because it comes from God; the required behavior is motivated transcendentally because it is taught by God; the manifestation of kindness to non-Christians is motivated transcendentally because God first demonstrated kindness toward the Cretans when they were unsaved. There is therefore, nothing "ordinary" about what is required from the Cretan believers. On the contrary, the false teaching encourages behavior that makes no real distinction between believers and unbelievers.

Contiguous Development; or, The Principle of Contiguity between Dominant Objectives

The overall rhetorical strategy may also be approached from another angle, not in terms of the chronological development of the argument as outlined above, but *in terms of the commonalities between the dominant rhetorical objectives*. In terms of this approach, four different (but related) rhetorical objectives can be identified.

Paul's first objective is to *persuade the Cretans of the need to recognize legitimate ministry*. This he does in units 1 (1:1–4), 2 (1:5–9), 4 (2:1), and 11 (3:12–15). He begins by trying to convince the audience of the legitimacy of teachers and their teaching. In unit 1 (1:1–4), he presents himself as a legitimate teacher by arguing on the basis of *divine authorization*. To this end, he *adapts the salutation to emphasize the divine basis of legitimate ministry*, which includes the legitimization both of the doctrine and the teacher. The same unit also includes *apostolic authorization* of the ministry of Titus. Unit 2 (1:1–4) sees the delegation of authority to Titus who is authorized to appoint local leaders. The dominant rhetorical objective of this unit is to *specify the criteria for legitimate local leadership*. In unit 4 (2:1), the dominant rhetorical objective is *to distinguish Titus on the basis of apostolic authorization, as a minister of sound doctrine* from the illegitimate teachers of unit 3 (1:10–16). In unit 11 (3:12–15), Paul adapts the conclusion *to reemphasize the notion of legitimate ministry* by the introduction of Tychicus, Artemis, Zenas, and Apollos, who are examples of apostolically authorized ministers of the church. Thus, in these four units we have three levels of authorization of legitimate ministry: of Paul by God; of Titus, Artemis or Tychicus, Zenas, and Apollos by Paul; and of the elder overseers by Titus. These units, collectively, convey the notion that the teaching ministry in the church is not for any ambitious Tom, Dick, and Harry: there are clear guidelines that must be satisfied with respect to those who teach as well as regards the content of their teaching.

The second objective is to *highlight God's central role as the Author of sound doctrine, the Teacher of sound doctrine, and the Model of good deeds*. Three key units express this objective, namely units 1 (1:1–4), 6 (2:11–15), and 9 (3:4–7). Each of these units consists of a single sentence, and each one focuses almost exclusively on the role of God. In unit 1 (1:1–4), the dominant rhetorical objective involved *adapting the salutation to emphasize the divine basis of legitimate ministry*. At one level, the unit introduces the notion of the legitimization of ministry. At another level, it also introduces the notion of the divine authorship of sound doctrine, which is presented as the manifestation of "God's word" (ἐφανέρωσεν . . . τὸν λόγον αὐτοῦ) (1:3). In this way, Paul establishes from the outset the following notion: "What I'm presenting to you is God's word. Titus, the elder overseers, and other legitimate teachers will do the same. Sound doctrine is sound because sound doctrine is God's word." In unit 6 (2:11–15), the dominant rhetorical objective was described as *emphasizing the divine basis of obedience to sound doctrine*. It communicates the following notion: "When you adjust your behavior, so that it complies with sound doctrine, you are really showing your obedience to God rather than to humanity, because God is the real teacher of sound doctrine." The dominant rhetorical objective of unit 9 (3:4–7) is *to persuade the Cretans that conformity to the example of God is the reason for displaying good works to those considered to be undeserving*. It communicates the following notion: "What are you doing? Don't you understand you are most like God when you practice good deeds for those whom you do not consider worthy? Then you are following God's example. Decide whose example you want to follow!"

The third objective is *to alienate the Cretans from any apparent or potential allegiance to unhealthy doctrine and its propagators*. This is addressed in units 3 (1:10–16) and 10 (3:8–11). In unit 3, the dominant rhetorical objective is *to discredit the illegitimate teachers* through the rhetorical technique of *vilification*. It communicates the notion that illegitimate teachers must be avoided since they are neither divinely nor apostolically authorized to minister to the church. Unit 10 (3:8–11) reemphasizes the notion of illegitimate teaching by contrasting it with sound doctrine. The dominant rhetorical objective can be summarized as *reinforcing the differences between sound and illegitimate doctrine in order to encourage compliance to the former and rejection of the latter*. The rhetorical technique of *vilification* is utilized again, but this time the emphasis is upon the vilification of *both* the unsound doctrine as well as the promoter thereof.

The fourth objective is *to emphasize the relationship between sound doctrine and behavior consequential to the doctrine*. This happens in units 5 (2:2–10), 7 (3:1–2), 8 (3:3), and 10 (3:8–11). In unit 5 (2:2–10), the dominant rhetorical objective is *to persuade the Cretans that personal conduct compliant with sound doctrine is compulsory and should characterize all believers*. The notion the apostle seems to communicate can be summarized as follows: "Sound doctrine from sound teachers should manifest as sound behavior among all believers." This unit follows the description of the illegitimate teachers who "profess to know God but deny God by their deeds" (1:16). Unit 7 (3:1–2) expresses the following dominant rhetorical objective, namely *to persuade the Cretans of the compulsory treatment of all unbelievers in a manner consistent with sound doctrine*. It conveys the following notion: "Sound doctrine ought to make model citizens of you. Even the rest of society expects this from you." In unit 8 (3:3), the dominant rhetorical objective was summarized as follows: *evoking disgust with past sinful behavior in order to reinforce behavior in the present that complies with sound doctrine*. The notion it conveys can be summarized as follows: "Expecting you to behave in a civil manner toward those whom you consider unworthy is not unreasonable. In fact, it is but another opportunity to manifest the doctrine we believe. Don't forget, we were all once undeserving brutes." In unit 10 (3:8–11), the dominant rhetorical objective is described as *reinforcing the differences between sound and illegitimate doctrine in order to encourage compliance to the former and rejection of the latter.* It conveys the following notion: "This doctrine is proven. I, Paul confirm this to be true, and if you obey it you can only benefit. It will prove that you really believe in God."

These four objectives may be summarized as follows:

First objective: Convince the audience of the need to recognize legitimate forms of ministry (units 1 [1:1–4], 2 [1:1–4], 4 [2:1], and 11 [3:12–15]).

Second objective: Convince the audience of God's central role as the Author of sound doctrine, the Teacher of sound doctrine, and the Model of good deeds (units 1 [1:1–4]), 6 [2:11–15], and 9 [3:4–7]).

Third objective: Convince the audience to alienate themselves from any apparent or potential allegiance to unhealthy doctrine and its propagators (units 3 [1:10–16] and 10 [3:8–11]).

Fourth objective: Convince the audience of the relationship between sound doctrine and behavior consequential to the doctrine (units 5 [2:2–10], 7 [3:1–2], 8 [3:3], and 10 [3:8–11]).

The discussion above shows how this study contributes a unique and distinct description of the overall rhetorical strategy of the Letter to Titus. It presupposes the existence of rhetorical strategies within the text and has identified and described the author's rhetorical strategy from the text itself, not only section by section, but also in terms of overall strategy and recurrent objectives. There is, to my knowledge, no other study of this nature that utilizes this methodology and applies it in particular to the Letter to Titus. It is presented as *a* method, rather than a panacea. Its major value lies in addressing the coherency debate by suggesting a multilayered coherent structure for this Cinderella letter.

Appendix

Text-generated persuasion analysis brought to the surface various *types of arguments* employed in the letter. In this regard, the following can be identified:

1. *Arguments based on the notion of divine authorization*

    Arguments based on the notion of divine authorization are foundational for the apostle's rhetorical strategy in this letter. It is by far the most frequently used type of argument in this letter (followed by arguments based on shared knowledge—see next section). In a letter of this nature that deals with issues of legitimacy and the challenge of illegitimacy, it is important to establish the basis of legitimacy. It is, therefore, significant that the apostle's first objective is to convince the Cretans of the divine basis of legitimate ministry. Since the church is God's elect, (ἐκλεκετοί θεοῦ), God has a right to prescribe who may or may not minister to them. Equally important is the second dominant rhetorical objective, which sets out to convince the Cretans of God's central role as the Author of sound doctrine, the Teacher of sound doctrine, and the Model of good deeds. Related to this is the concept that God expects a particular behavior from those who profess to believe in God. Hence, any failure to behave in a manner compliant to sound doctrine is presented as tantamount to a denial of God (1:16). Also, in 2:2–10, the negligent behavior of believers can either be a cause for God's word to be maligned, or God's doctrine can be adorned by sound conduct. Similarly, the reference to Cretans as "those who believe in God" (οἱ πεπιστευκότες θεῷ) is another variation of this kind of argument that God expects a particular behavior from those who believe in God. Following on from this is a further variation of the divine authorization argument, namely *the divine prerogative* or *the right of the divine.* This argument is closely related to the argument of the divine expectation of a particular behavior. According to 2:11-15, God has a right over those whom God has redeemed (λυτρόομαι) and cleansed (καθαρίζω) from all lawlessness (ἀπὸ πάσης ἀνομίας). Since God is the one who purchased and cleansed the Cretan believers, they belong to God; hence the prerogative to prescribe the appropriate behavior belongs to God.

Furthermore, this line of argumentation is foundational for the past, present, and future momentum characteristic of this letter. There is a hope (ἐλπίς), but only those who behave in the divinely expected manner can look forward to it. Negatively, this implies that those who deviate from the expected behavior can anticipate the opposite of what the obedient ones are expecting.

2. *Arguments based on shared knowledge*

Arguments based on shared knowledge employ accepted societal norms regarding proper and acceptable behavior as a legitimate yardstick of behavior. The virtue and vice lists pertaining to elder overseers and illegitimate teachers respectively (1:5-9, 10-16) are examples of this kind of argument. It is also used in 2:2-10 with regard to the conduct of believers, as well as in 3:1-3. Paul uses these arguments to convince the Cretans of the necessity to behave in a manner compliant with sound doctrine, which will reflect behavior considered admirable by society. Negatively, this kind of argument serves to present the false teachers in a bad light by highlighting the extent to which their conduct contradicts the positive behavior that society in general upholds. This line of argumentation makes it very difficult for the Cretans not to conduct themselves in a manner compliant with the sound doctrine. Its persuasive power also lies in the fact that the commendable conduct is obvious and known to all.

3. *Arguments based on the existence of prior knowledge or based on the appeal to memory*

Paul uses an argument based on the appeal to his audience's memory or prior knowledge in 3:1-3. This kind of argumentation presents the audience with an opportunity for a subjective evaluation of the information presented to them. They can evaluate the consistency of the doctrine because they are not expected to comprehend new information. They are called to act in ways they have known to be consistent with sound doctrine. On the negative side, a refusal to act consistently with what they have known to be true would amount to a moral paradox, thus making this line of argumentation very persuasive.

4. *Arguments based on the notion of irreconcilable conduct*

The salutation lays the groundwork for this line of argumentation when the church is referred to as ἐκλεκτοί θεοῦ, whose faith and knowledge of the truth must be for the goal of conforming to godliness (εὐσέβεια). Thus, godliness will characterize the ἐκλεκτοί θεοῦ. An ungodly ἐκλεκτός θεοῦ would be unthinkable or irreconcilable.

In 2:11–14, Paul describes the Cretans as God's own possession, zealous for good works (ἑαυτῷ λαὸν περιούσιον ζηλωτὴν καλῶν ἔργων). The argument is as follows: those who belong to God are zealous for good works, Cretan believers belong to God, and therefore the Cretan believers are zealous for good works. Negatively, this argument contends that the absence of a zeal for good works is tantamount to not belonging to God. It is thus a form of irreconcilable conduct to belong to God and not to be zealous for good works.

The reference to the believers in 3:8 as φροντίζωσιν καλῶν ἔργων προΐστασθαι οἱ πεπιστευκότες θεῷ is another instance of this line of argumentation. To believe in God and not engage in good deeds would also constitute irreconcilable conduct.

5. *Arguments based upon identification with the audience*

In 3:3, the apostle argues on the basis of *identification with his audience* in order to achieve his objective of engendering a compliant attitude. This technique provides the apostle with a platform from which to address his audience, effectively reinforcing his authority and right to speak to them with great liberty and confidence.

6. *Arguments based on the use of vilification of the opposition*

Vilification is a technique that Paul uses very effectively to influence the perception of his audience regarding the opposition. In units 3 (1:10–16) and 10 (3:8–11), he sets out to persuade his audience concerning the illegitimacy of the doctrine of the opposition. The intention is to get the audience to change their minds about the false teachers and their teaching by raising doubts concerning their character and their teaching. For example, he refers to their teaching as "things" (ἃ) (1:11) while the quote in 1:12 is used to cast doubt upon the character of the false teachers, being ψεῦσται κακὰ θηρία γαστέρες ἀργαί.

Lastly, attention should be focused on the *wide range of rhetorical techniques employed* in the Letter to Titus. Most of these techniques are well known and are listed here for reference purposes. (In the analysis sections their function has already been discussed.) Furthermore, four additional techniques have been pointed out in this study, which seem not to have been identified by scholars thus far. They will be highlighted briefly in the second half of this review.

1. Rhetorical techniques used most often in the letter include:

    a. Paronomasia: for example κοσμικὰς (2:12) and κοσμῶσιν (2:10).

    b. Implicit contrasting: An example of this technique occurs in chapter 1 with the positive description of the elder overseers (vv. 5-9) followed by a description of the false teachers (vv. 10-16). The contrast between the two groups is implicit rather than explicit, since there are no indications of a simile being drawn. A more subtle example is the comparison between the character of God and that of the false teachers in 1:2 and 1:12 respectively. God is described as being "unlying" (ἀψευδὴς) while the false teachers are called "always liars" (ἀεὶ ψεῦσται).

    c. Personification: For example, in 2:12 grace is said to instruct the believers (παιδεύουσα ἡμᾶς).

    d. Asyndeton: For example, in 3:1-2 a variety of nouns and infinitives are paired without the use of conjunctions: ἀρχαῖς ἐξουσίαις ὑποτάσσεσθαι πειθαρχεῖν, πρὸς πᾶν ἔργον ἀγαθὸν ἑτοίμους εἶναι μηδένα βλασφημεῖν, ἀμάχους εἶναι ἐπιεικεῖς, πᾶσαν ἐνδεικνυμένους πραΰτητα πρὸς πάντας ἀνθρώπους.

    e. Syndeton: For example, in 3:4: ἡ χρηστότης καὶ φιλανθρωπία.

    f. Polysyndeton: For example, in 3:9: μωρὰς δὲ ζητήσεις καί ἔρεις καὶ μάχας νομικὰς. In this example, the technique functions to create the impression of endless list of useless topics.

    g. Repetitions: For example, in 1:9 one finds τῇ διδασκαλίᾳ ὑγιαινούσῃ and 2:1 τῇ ὑγιαινούσῃ διδασκαλίᾳ.

h. Metaphor: For example, in 1:4 Titus is called Paul's "true child," a metaphorical reference to family life. In 3:14 we find an agricultural reference to fruitlessness, ἄκαρποι.

i. Inclusive language: For example, in 3:3: Ἦμεν γάρ ποτε καὶ ἡμεῖς.

j. Synonyms: For example, in 1:16 we encounter ἔργον ἀγαθὸν. In 2:7 we find καλῶν ἔργων.

k. Antonyms: For example, in 1:2: ἀψευδής and in 1:12, ψεῦσται.

l. Them/us language: For example, in 1:12: τίς ἐξ αὐτῶν ἴδιος αὐτῶν προφήτης.

m. Example: For example, in 3:4–7 God is presented as an example of one who shows kindness to those who do not deserve it. According to 1:2, God does not lie. Paul, as a servant of God (1:1), is also an example to others, who are in master-servant relationships (2:9).

n. Chiasm: For example, in 1:3–4, we find the following references to God and Jesus Christ:

| A—τοῦ σωτῆρος | B—ἡμῶν θεοῦ (1:3) |
| B*—Χρισοῦ Ἰησοῦ | A*—τοῦ σωτῆρος ἡμῶν (1:4) |

In 3:4 and 3:6 we find the same:

| A—τοῦ σωτῆρος | B—ἡμῶν θεοῦ (3:4) |
| B*—Ἰησοῦ Χριστοῦ | A*—τοῦ σωτῆρος ἡμῶν (3:6) |

In 1:15 we find another example, with a slight variation, viz. AABA:

| A—πάντα καθαρὰ | A—τοῖς καθαροῖς |
| B*—τοῖς δὲ μεμιαμμένοις καὶ ἀπίστοις | A*—οὐδὲν καθαρόν |

o. Transitional devices: For example, section 1:5–9 deals with the elder overseers, but in verse 9, which describes the responsibility of the elder overseers, the false teachers are introduced as τοὺς ἀντιλέγοντας, just before the next section (1:10–16) in which they are fully dealt with. This small word, in 1:9, thus functions as a transitional device that introduces the next section.

p. Anaphora: For example, in 1:8: φιλόξενον and φιλάγαθον, and in 2:4: φιλάνδρους ... φιλοτέκνους.

q. Assonance: For example, in 2:11 the rhyming and repetition of the ως sound in σωφρόνως καὶ δικαίως καὶ εὐσεβῶς.

r. Thematic progression: For example, the theme of servanthood is developed starting with Paul as an obedient servant of God, while slaves must submit to their own masters (2:9). Related to this is the theme of submission to authority: wives to their husbands (2:5), servants to their masters (2:9), and believers to secular authorities (3:1). Thus, submission starts in the home, then moves to the place of employment, and finally occurs within secular society.

s. Alliteration and rhyme: For example, in 3:3: δουλεύοντες ... διάγοντες.

t. Anthropopathism: For example, in 3:4–7 the reference to God's kindness and love for humanity (χρηστότης καὶ φιλανθρωπία) (v. 4) and mercy (ἔλεος) (v. 5).

u. Unusually long sentences: For example, 1:1–4, 2:11–14, and 3:4–7.

v. Unusually short sentences: For example, 1:13, 2:15b, and 3:8.

w. Synecdoche: For example, in 3:10, the reference to the opposition in the singular as αἱρετικός ἄνθρωπος.

x. Homoioteleuton: For example, 1:1: Παῦλος δοῦλος ... ἀπόστολος and θεοῦ ... Ἰησοῦ Χριστοῦ. The endings are similar, which heightens the emphatic value of the first line of the opening sentence.

2. New rhetorical techniques that have been identified are:

a. *Emphatic clustering*

This technique is used in several places in the letter. There are variations of the technique, namely asyndetic (1:12; 2:2) and polysyndetic clustering (1:16; 2:12, 15).

The device involves the grouping together or clustering of related concepts or words in groups of three. Clustering serves an emphatic purpose. In chapter 1, it is employed as part of the apostle's vilification campaign in 1:10, 12, and 16 highlighting the "badness" of the false teachers. In 2:2, it is used to emphasize the sound behavior expected of older men. In 2:7, it is used to impress upon Titus what is required from him as an example to the believers. In 2:12, the conduct of those who are instructed by grace is emphasized by the words σωφρόνως καὶ εὐσεβῶς. In 2:15, it is used to impress upon Titus the urgency with which he must approach his ministry (λάλει καὶ παρακάλει καὶ ἔλεγχε). A final instance of this technique appears in 3:11, which constitutes a final instance of vilification.

b. *Self-vilification*
This rhetorical technique is used in 3:3 with reference to the pre-salvific conduct of the believers. The list of vices is used to instill disgust. Here, it is not the opponents that are being vilified, but Paul and the believers, by Paul. It highlights the odiousness of their past life and is used to enforce compliance to behavior that corresponds to sound doctrine.

c. *Honorific referencing or classification*
This technique is the opposite of vilification or more specifically, self-vilification. Paul refers to believers in ways that emphasize their privileged status, thus bestowing honor upon them. This strategy is utilized to build relationships. Thus, believers are called ἐκλεκτοί θεοῦ (1:1), οἱ πεπιστευκότες θεῷ (3:8), οἱ ἡμέτεροι (3:13), and τοὺς φιλοῦντας ἡμᾶς ἐν πίστει (3:15).

d. *Networks created by the repetition of associated concepts*
In the analysis section, it has been pointed out how various related words or concepts are repeated in different units and in different contexts. This technique makes several processes possible. One of these is implicit contrasting, which is facilitated merely through the repetition of a cognate word within a different context. This technique also facilitates the remarkable coherency that is evident within the letter. An outstanding example is the instance of paronomasia associated with the following words: ἀνυπότακτα (Christian children of elder overseers), ἀνυπότακτοι (false teachers), ὑποτασσομένας (Christian young women), ὑποτάσσεσθαι (Christian slaves). The word ὑποτασσω and its cognates contrast the opposing groups within the letter and establish a network of positive behavior shared by those who are associated with sound doctrine.

e. *Implicit contrasting*
Words used in a specific context are repeated in a subsequent context in order to link the two contexts and contrast the two. E.g., the expression, πρὸς πᾶν ἔργον ἀγαθὸν ἑτοίμους εἶναι (3:1), which but for the infinitive and the adjective, is an exact replication of an earlier prepositional phrase: πρὸς πᾶν ἔργον ἀγαθὸν ἀδόκιμοι (1:16). However, in the earlier appearance it referred to false teachers while in the latter appearance it applies to believers. The contrast is therefore implicit rather than explicit. Another instance occurs when God is described as ἀψευδὴς (1:2) while the Cretans are referred to as ψεῦσται (1:12).

This study has led me to a new appreciation for the rhetorical genius of the apostle Paul. Furthermore, it offers, almost serendipitously so, fresh perspectives beneficial for the authenticity debate. The implications of the cumulative-complimentary reading principle certainly have potential for further investigation. In terms of practical theology, the homiletical benefit of text-generated persuasion analysis is another area that holds rich dividends for further study. Indeed, anything that will help the church with the persuasive proclamation of the gospel warrants our attention.

The message of this letter to Titus may not be considered as unique, but the way in which it is communicated certainly is. Indeed, this little letter does not need to stand in the shadow of the Timothean correspondence.

Bibliography

Achtemeier, P. J., J. B. Green, and M. M. Thompson. *Introducing the New Testament: Its Literature and Theology*. Grand Rapids, MI: Eerdmans, 2001.

Amador, J. D. H. "Where Could Rhetorical Criticism (Still) Take Us?" *Currents in Research: Biblical Studies* 7 (1999) 195–222.

Anderson, R. D. *Ancient Rhetorical Theory and Paul: Contributions to Biblical Exegesis and Theology*. Kampen: Kok Pharos, 1996.

Bailey, M. L. "A Theology of Paul's Pastoral Epistles." In *A Biblical Theology of the New Testament*, edited by R. B. Zuck and D. L. Bock. Chicago: Moody Press, 1994.

Bauer, F. C. *Die Sogennanten Pastoralbriefe Des Apostels Paulus*. Stuttgart and Tübingen: Gottaschen Verlagshandlung, 1835.

Becker, S. L. "Rhetorical Scholarship in the Seventies." In *Rhetoric: A Tradition in Transition: In Honor of Donald C. Bryant*, edited by Walter R. Fisher. East Lansing: Michigan State University Press, 1974.

Bernard, J. H. *The Pastoral Epistles: Timothy and Titus*. Ada, MI: Baker, 1980.

Betz, H. D. *Galatians: A Commentary on Paul's Letter to the Churches in Galatia*. Hermeneia: A Critical and Historical Commentary on the Bible. Philadelphia: Fortress, 1979.

Boonzaaier, J. B. "Vilifikasie: 'n Nuwe Kyk Op Die Bedreiging Van Kolossense." *H. T. S. Theological Studies* 59, no. 4 (2003) 1259–86.

Botha, P. J. J. "The Verbal Art of the Pauline Letters: Rhetoric, Performance and Presence." In *Rhetoric and the New Testament: Essays from the 1992 Heidelberg Conference*, edited by S. E. Porter and T. H. Olbricht, 409–28. Sheffield: Sheffield Academic, 1993.

Bowman, R. M., Jr. "Jesus Christ, God Manifest: Titus 2:13 Revisited." *Journal of the Evangelical Theological Society* 51, no. 4 (2008) 733–52.

Burke, K. *A Rhetoric of Motives*. New York: Prentice-Hall, 1950.

Carson, D. A., and D. J. Moo. *An Introduction to the New Testament*. Grand Rapids, MI: Zondervan, 2005.

Clark, D. J. "Discourse Structure in Titus." *Technical Papers for the Bible Translator* 53, no. 1 (2002) 101–17.

Classen, C. J. *Rhetorical Criticism of the New Testament*. Leiden: Brill Academic, 2002.

———. "A Rhetorical Reading of the Epistle to Titus." *Journal for the Study of the New Testament Supplement Series* (1997) 427–44.

Collins, R. F. "The Theology of the Epistle to Titus." *Ephemerides Theologicae Lovanienses* Tomus 76, no. 76 (2000) 56–72.

———. *1 and 2 Timothy and Titus: A Commentary*. Louisville, KY: Westminster John Knox, 2002.
D'Angelo, F. J. "Rhetorical Criticism." In *Encyclopedia of Rhetoric and Composition: Communication from Ancient Times to the Information Age*, edited by Theresa Enos, 604–8. New York: Garland, 1996.
Davies, M. *The Pastoral Epistles*. Sheffield: Sheffield Academic, 1996.
Demarest, G. *1 and 2 Thessalonians, 1 and 2 Timothy, Titus*. Waco, TX: Word Books, 1984.
Dibelius, M., and H. Conzelmann. *The Pastoral Epistles: A Commentary on the Pastoral Epistles*. Philadelphia: Fortress, 1972.
Dio Chrysostom. *Discourses*. Edited by T. E. Page, translated by J. W. Cohoon. 2nd ed. 5 vols. Loeb Classical Library. Cambridge, MA: Harvard University Press, 1932–51.
Donelson, L. *Pseudipigraphy and Ethical Argument in the Pastoral Epistles*. Vol. 67. Tübingen: Mohr-Siebeck, 1986.
Du Toit, A. B. "Alienation and Re-Identification as Pragmatic Strategies in Galatians." *Neotestamentica* 26, no. 2 (1992) 279–95.
———. "Persuasion in Romans 1:1–17." *Biblische Zeitschrift* 33, no. 2 (1989) 192–209.
———. "Vilification as a Pragmatic Device in Early Christian Epistolography." *Biblica* 75, no. 3 (1994) 403–12.
Dunn, J. D. G. *The First and Second Letters to Timothy and the Letter to Titus*. Nashville, TN: Abingdon, 2000.
Easton, B. S. *The Pastoral Epistles*. London: SCM Press, 1948.
Eichorn, J. G. *Einleitung in Das Neuen Testament*. Leipzig: Weidemannischen Buchhandlung, 1812.
Epp, E. J., and G. W. MacRae, eds. *The New Testament and Its Modern Interpreters*. The Bible and Its Modern Interpreters, edited by D. A. Knight. Atlanta, GA: Scholars Press, 1989.
Evanson, E. *The Dissonance of the Four Generally Received Evangelists, and the Evidence of Their Respective Authenticity Examined; with That of Some Other Scriptures Deemed Canonical*. Gloucester: D. Walker for J. Johnson, 1805.
Faber, R. " 'Evil Beasts, Lazy Gluttons': A Neglected Theme in the Epistle to Titus." *Westminster Journal of Theology*, no. 67 (2005) 135–45.
Fee, G. D. *1 and 2 Timothy, Titus*. New International Biblical Commentary. Peabody, MA: Hendrickson, 1988.
———. *Pauline Christology: An Exegetical-Theological Study*. Peabody, MA: Hendrickson, 2007.
Fiore, B. *The Function of Personal Example in the Socratic and Pastoral Epistles*. Rome: Rome Biblical Institute Press, 1986.
Gill, D. W. J. "A Saviour for the Cities of Crete: The Roman Background for the Epistle to Titus." In *The New Testament in Its First Century Setting: Essays on Context and Background in Honour of B. W. Winter on His 65th Birthday*, edited by P. J. Williams, A. D. Clark, P. M. Head, and D. Instone-Brewer. Grand Rapids, MI: Eerdmans, 2004.
Gray, P. "The Liar Paradox and the Letter to Titus." *Catholic Biblical Quarterly* 69, no. 2 (2007) 302–14.
Guthrie, D. *The Pastoral Epistles*. Edited by R. V. Tasker. The Tyndale New Testament Commentaries. London: Tyndale, 1957.

Bibliography 133

Hagner, D. A. "Titus as a Pauline Letter." In *Society of Biblical Literature 1998 Seminar Papers Part Two*, 546-58. Atlanta, GA: Scholars Press, 1998.

Hanson, A. T. *Studies in the Pastoral Epistles*. London: SPCK, 1968.

Harding, M. *Tradition and Rhetoric in the Pastoral Epistles*. New York: Peter Lang, 1998.

Harris, M. J. "Titus 2:13 and the Deity of Christ: Pauline Studies." In *Essays Presented to Professor F. F. Bruce on His 70th Birthday*, edited by D. A. Hagner and M. J. Harris, 263-73. Grand Rapids, MI: Eerdmans, 1980.

Harvey, J. D. *Listening to the Text: Oral Patterning in Paul's Letters*. Grand Rapids, MI: Baker Books, 1998.

Hendriksen, W. *1 and 2 Timothy and Titus*. London: Banner of Truth Trust, 1957.

Hester, J. D., and J. D. Hester (Amador), eds. *Rhetorics and Hermeneutics: Wilhelm Wuellner and His Influence*. Edited by V. K. Robbins. Emory Studies in Early Christianity. London: T&T Clark, 2004.

Hester (Amador), J. D. "The Wuellnerian Sublime: Rhetorics, Power and the Ethics of Commun(icat)ion." In *Emory Studies in Early Christianity*, edited by V. K. Robbins. London: T&T Clark, 2004.

Hultgren, A. J. *1-2 Timothy, Titus*. Minneapolis, MN: Augsburg, 1984.

Johnson, L. T. *Letters to Paul's Delegates: 1 Timothy, 2 Timothy, Titus*. Valley Forge, PA: Trinity, 1996.

Karris, R. J. *The Pastoral Epistles*, edited by W. Harrington and D. Senior. Vol. 17, *New Testament Message: A Biblical Theological Commentary*. Wilmington, DE: Michael Glazier, 1979.

———. *A Symphony of New Testament Hymns: Commentary on Philippians 2:5-11, Colossians 1:15-20, Ephesians 2:14-16, 1 Timothy 3:16, Titus 3:4-7, 1 Peter 3:18-22, and 2 Timothy 2:11-13*. Collegeville, MN: Liturgical Press, 1996.

Kelly, J. N. D. *A Commentary on the Pastoral Epistles 1 Timothy, 2 Timothy, Titus*. London: A&C Black, 1960.

Kennedy, G. A. *New Testament Interpretation through Rhetorical Criticism*. Chapel Hill: University of North Carolina Press, 1984.

Kidd, R. M. "Titus as Apologia: Grace for Liars Beasts and Bellies." *Horizons in Biblical Theology* 21, no. 2 (1999) 185-209.

Knight, G. W., III. *The Pastoral Epistles: A Commentary on the Greek Text*. Grand Rapids, MI: Eerdmans, 1992.

Köstenberger, A. J. "Hermeneutical and Exegetical Challenges in Interpreting the Pastoral Epistles." *The Southern Baptist Journal of Theology* 7, no. 3 (2003) 4-17.

Lambrecht, J. *Pauline Studies: Collected Essays*. Vol. 115, *Bibliotheca Ephemeridum Theologicarum Lovaniensium*. Leuven, Belgium: Leuven University Press, 1994.

Luther, Martin. "Preface to the Epistle of St. Paul to Titus." In *Luther's Works*. Vol. 35, *Word and Sacrament I*, edited by E. T. Bachmann. Philadelphia: Fortress, 1960.

Mappes, D. A. "Moral Virtues Associated with Eldership." *Bibliotheca Sacra* 160 (2003) 202-18.

Marshall, I. H. *A Critical and Exegetical Commentary on the Pastoral Epistles*. The International Critical Commentary on the Holy Scripture of the Old and New Testaments, edited by J. A. Emerton, C. E. B. Cranfield, and G. N. Stanton. London: T&T Clark, 2004.

———. "Some Recent Commentaries on the Pastoral Epistles." *Expository Times* 117, no. 4 (2006) 140-43.

Marshall, I. H., S. Travis, and I. Paul. *Exploring the New Testament: A Guide to the Letters and Revelation.* Vol. 2. Downers Grove, IL: InterVarsity, 2002.

Marshall, J. W. " 'I Left You in Crete': Narrative Deception and Social Hierarchy in the Letter to Titus." *Journal of Biblical Literature* 127, no. 4 (2008) 781–803.

McKnight, S., and G. R. Osborne. *The Face of New Testament Studies: A Survey of Recent Research.* Grand Rapids, MI: Baker Academic, 2004.

McRay, J. *Paul: His Life and Teaching.* Grand Rapids, MI: Baker Academic, 2003.

Meynet, R. *Rhetorical Analysis: An Introduction to Biblical Rhetoric.* Sheffield: Sheffield Academic, 1998.

Miller, J. D. "The Pastoral Letters as Composite Documents." In *Society for New Testament Studies: Monograph Series,* edited by R. Bauckham. Cambridge: Cambridge University Press, 1997.

Mounce, W. D. *Pastoral Epistles.* Nashville, TN: Thomas Nelson, 2000.

Oden, T. C. *First and Second Timothy and Titus.* Louisville, KY: John Knox, 1989.

Olbricht, T. H. "Rhetorical Criticism in Biblical Commentaries." *Currents in Biblical Research* 7, no. 11 (2008) 11–36.

Orton, D. E., and R. D. Anderson, eds. *Handbook of the Literary Rhetoric: A Foundation for Literary Study.* Leiden: Brill, 1998.

Porter, S. E. "The Theoretical Justification for Application of Rhetorical Categories to Pauline Epistolary Literature." In *Rhetoric and the New Testament,* 100–22. Sheffield: JSOT Press, 1993.

Porter, S. E., and T. H. Olbricht. *Rhetoric, Scripture and Theology: Essays from the 1994 Pretoria Conference,* Journal for the Study of the New Testament. Sheffield: Sheffield Academic, 1996.

Porter, S., and D. L. Stamps, eds. *Rhetorical Criticism and the Bible.* Journal for the Study of the New Testament Supplement Series. London: Sheffield Academic, 2002.

———. *The Rhetorical Interpretation of Scripture: Essays from the 1996 Malibu Conference,* Journal for the Study of the New Testament Supplement Series. London: Sheffield Academic, 1999.

Quinn, J. D. *The Letter to Titus: A New Translation with Notes and Commentary and an Introduction to Titus, 1 Timothy, and the Pastoral Epistles.* New York: Doubleday, 1990.

Richards, J. *Rhetoric.* The New Critical Idiom, edited by John Drakakis. London: Routledge, 2008.

Robbins, V. K. "Rhetorical Analysis of Biblical Documents in the Past Decade with Special Focus on the Seven 'Pepperdine' Conferences." Paper presented at the Heidelberg Conference on Rhetoric, Ethic, and Moral Persuasion in Biblical Discourse. Moore Haus of the Pepperdine University, Heidelberg, Germany, July 22–25, 2002.

Schleiermacher, F. E. D. *Über Den Ersten Brief Pauli an Timotheus.* Braunschweig/Leipzig: Gerhard Reuter, 1897.

Schmidt, J. E. C. *Historisch Kritische Einleitung In's Neue Testament,* 1804.

Simpson, E. K. *The Pastoral Epistles: The Greek Text with Introduction and Commentary.* London: Tyndale, 1954.

Smith, K. G. "The Structure of Titus: Criss-Cross Chiasmus as Structural Marker." *Conspectus: The Journal of the South African Theological Seminary* 3 (2007) 98–110.

Smith, K. G., and A. Song. "Some Christological Implications in Titus 2:13." *Neotestamentica* 40, no. 2 (2006) 284–94.

Smithson, A. "Grace and the Character of God." *Expository Times* 115, no. 3 (2003) 73–76.

Snyman, A. H. "Philippians 4:10–23 from a Rhetorical Perspective." *Acta Theologica* 27, no. 2 (2007) 168–85.

Thurston, B. B. "The Theology of Titus." *Horizons in Biblical Theology* 21, no. 2 (1999) 171–84.

Tollefson, K. D. "Titus: Epistle of Religious Revitalization." *Biblical Theology Bulletin* 30, no. 4 (2000) 145.

Tolmie, D. F. *Persuading the Galatians: A Text-Centred Rhetorical Analysis of a Pauline Letter*. Tübingen: Möhr Siebeck, 2005.

Towner, P. H. *The Goal of Our Instruction: The Structure of Theology and Ethics in the Pastoral Epistles*. Sheffield: Sheffield Academic, 1989.

———. *1–2 Timothy and Titus*. Leichester, UK: InterVarsity, 1994.

Van Neste, R. "The Message of Titus: An Overview." *Southern Baptist Journal of Theology* 7, no. 3 (2003) 18–30.

———. "Structure and Cohesion in Titus: Problems and Method." *Bible Translator* 53, no. 1 (2002) 118–33.

Verner, D. C. *The Household of God: The Social World of the Pastoral Epistles*. Chico, CA: Scholars Press, 1983.

Wallace, D. B. *Greek Grammar beyond the Basics: An Exegetical Syntax of the New Testament with Scripture, Subject and Greek Word Index*. Grand Rapids, MI: Zondervan, 1996.

Welch, Kathleen E. *The Contemporary Reception of Classical Rhetoric: Appropriations of Ancient Discourse*. London: Lawrence Erlbaum, 1990.

Wendland, E. R. " 'Let No One Disregard You!' (Titus 2:15): Church Discipline and the Construction of Discourse in a Personal, 'Pastoral' Epistle." In *Discourse Analysis and the New Testament: Approaches and Results*, edited by S. E. Porter and J. T. Reed, 334–51. Sheffield: Sheffield Academic, 1999.

Wieland, George M. "Grace Manifest: Missional Church in the Letter to Titus." *Stimulus* 13, no. 1 (2005) 8–11.

———. "Roman Crete and the Letter to Titus." *New Testament Studies* 55, no. 3 (2009) 338–54.

Witherington, B., III. *Letters and Homilies for Hellenized Christians*. Vol. 1, *A Socio-Rhetorical Commentary on Titus, 1–2 Timothy and 1–3 John*. Downers Grove, Nottingham: InterVarsity Academic, 2006.

Wuellner, W. "Where Is Rhetorical Criticism Taking Us?" *Catholic Biblical Quarterly* 49, no. 3 (1987) 448–63.

Zodhiates, S. *The Complete Word Study Dictionary: New Testament*. Chattanooga, TN: AMG, 1992.

www.ingramcontent.com/pod-product-compliance
Lightning Source LLC
Chambersburg PA
CBHW072151160426
43197CB00012B/2343